Fun Factory:

An Insider's Guide on the Video Game Industry

Ben Smedstad

Fun Factory: An Insider's Guide on the Video Game Industry

First published in Great Britain in 2017

By Forerunner Limited, www.forerunnerltd.com

Copyright 2017 Ben Smedstad

The right of Ben Smedstad to be identified as the author of this work as been asserted by him in accordance with the Copyright, Designs and Patents Act 1988

All rights reserved. No part of this publication may be reproduced, stored in a retrieval system, or transmitted, in any form or by any means, electronic, mechanical, photocopying, recording or otherwise, without the prior permission of the copyright owner.

All intellectual property and trademarks mentioned within this work are owned by their respective owners and are used by the author purely for context and narrative purposes.

ISBN 9781549506390

First Edition

Acknowledgements

Special thanks to Ray Muzyka and Greg Zeschuck for giving me a start in the industry, a journey that has become the centre of my life. Thanks to Laird Malamed for teaching me so much about making games and being a decent person while doing it. Thanks to Neil Postlethwaite for putting up with me and working together on so many things over the years but mostly for being my friend. Also, thanks to Trond Johansen and my wife for their generous feedback—making this book "readable" would not have been possible without them. I would also like to thank Kalvin Lyle for not only being a lifelong friend, but also for creating the cover art for this book.

Lastly and almost stereotypically but makes it no less true, many thanks to my wife, Lenore, for the years of patience, understanding and love.

Table of Contents

Acknowledgements 3

Forward: 6

Use your words. 8

The story so far: A VERY brief overview of games 13

From gamer to game maker: What's life like working in games? . 25

A gamers "office": Where you are when you are not sleeping 38

Production: The "behind-the-scenes" of behind-the-scenes people 47

Programming is magic - ask any programmer 57

Game Design: Who comes up with this "stuff"? 69

Knowing it when you see it: What is Art? 85

Marketing: Where toys and crazy ideas reside 99

QA: Gatekeepers and gamers 108

Audio: The other half of your gaming experience 116

Publisher and Developer relationships: Friendships and fistfights 125

So who pays for all this? How games get published 143

    The AAA game: Assessing the risks 151

"Hey, I have a great idea!": Where new projects come from 158

The life cycle of a AAA game: Putting it all together 163

Knowing gamers: It's a big, big gaming world out there.............184

Trolls, the community, and trying to make good things 190

Data, data, data - we need your data (or do we?).....................200

Making a splash, getting noticed: Tradeshows and PR................210

Times are changing: The death of the mid-range game..............226

Free to Play games: A new(er) way to make money...................242

Virtual and Augmented Reality: Are we there yet? How about now? Now? 253

Sounds great! I am in: Getting into the industry 264

But seriously, how do I get into the games industry?.................273

Endrant: The birth, life, and death of an indie studio 284

So, what did we learn? 318

Forward:

I remember Christmas, 1980 or 1981—my dad bought our first gaming system, an Atari 2600. Little did he know this was the start of my lifelong passion for gaming, and for a six year old, this was pretty much the coolest present. Whether it was *PAC-MAN*, *Space Invaders*, *Defender*, or *Pitfall!*, this was the genesis of gaming for a good chunk of the game developers you read about now. We cut our teeth on gaming by playing these titles when we were kids. This was the first real mass introduction to home gaming. You could play games from the arcade at home! You know how many bowling alleys and convenience stores lost quarters because of this device? Actually none. We still ventured out and dumped our allowances into those machines, but when we were broke, we headed home to play our Atari 2600s.

This time was also the birthplace for a large portion of the major video game publishers of today. Activision, Electronic Arts, and others were all started by ex-employees, splinter groups, and others who at one time worked for Atari or developed games for the Atari 2600 system. 30 million systems were sold and made home gaming a "thing", enough to become mainstream, and part of people's living rooms. It would have blown my little six year old mind to find out that years later I would be working with all these companies to create the next generation of entertainment.

This is when my whole life began to revolve around games. At the time I didn't know that gaming would become a long-term obsession, the thread that has woven through my entire 40+ years on the planet. Gaming will be still a part of my life in the far-flung future when I am in a retirement home—hopefully I will be hooked up to a Virtual Reality rig to continue exploring and playing games.

In this book I want to show you the behind-the-scenes of the games industry and how it works, and try providing a sense of the scope involved when making any game... whether the results are good or bad while holding back nothing. I will use anecdotes and lessons learned over the last 22+ years and 18 shipped games for context, and more than a few harrowing tales of warning. Name dropping, and inside stories of companies being born and dying all included.

Use your words.

In 2001 I was sitting in one of my first big meetings at a publisher. I had just started my new job as a producer at the biggest games publisher in the world, Activision. After six years working at game developer studios, I had my first real look at how publishers did things. I was excited and more than a bit nervous about showing off the game we were working on to the vice presidents of Marketing, Public Relations, and Production, and the actual President of Activision. Some of the most important people in the company, arguably of the video game industry as a whole, were reviewing and passing judgment on my work... directly to me, no filters!

The project's executive producer started with the summary: "We will try to keep the GL meeting short so we can review code. The RoW SKUs on the P&L were low on the worst case but decent on base case. The DD thought the schedule was off, and so the costs would be actually a bit higher, but the CD/PD disagreed. Add in that our TCRs and TRC failure rate was high and would need another several more re-subs to both MS and Sony - That's just doing EFIGs and box n' docs for the rest."

Did you follow that? I sure didn't at the time, and at least you don't have to stand up and speak next like you know what the hell they were talking about. Every industry has its share of terms and designations, and the games industry is particularly atrocious as it draws from both tech AND entertainment...with a ton of business terms and buzz words thrown in. Even more fun, each company has its own terms for the same things you recently learned somewhere else, because... reasons.

Now I am not going to try to teach you fine folks deep dive terms, but there are some basic key words and concepts that should be clearly defined. These terms will help you understand how a game developer is organized internally. Without this understanding you may get a bit lost[1].

What is a Developer?

A developer (usually abbreviated to *Dev*) are the people that actually make the game. They are programmers, artists, designers, sound engineers, and everyone else including the management, required to actually make the game. There are two basic categories:

---

[1] Sorry for the readers who knew these terms already but many people unfamiliar with the industry do not.

internal and external developers. I have seen the ratio of internal to external studios shift in cycles over the years. Recently as 2016, you see the vast majority of AAA games being made by internal studios, while in previous years (early 2000s) the majority were external. The reasons for this cycle vary but mostly revolves around risk, control and ultimately money.

Internal developers

Internal developers are production teams working for the publisher, funders, marketers and sales. The line where the developer starts and the publisher ends can be blurry in these situations. Many internal developers started out as external but were purchased by the publisher. How and why this happens can be for any number of reasons. Usually it's because the Dev did great producing a game or representing the intellectual property, and the publisher wants to lock them down permanently for more titles. It's as much about making sure their own franchises are treated well as depriving competition from good talent.

Infinity Ward was founded in 2002 as an independent developer working on the *Call of Duty* game. Activision helped set them up with a 30% ownership for investment, which basically said "hands off" to other publishers. The day after the release and confirmation of the game's success, Activision purchased the remaining 70% of the company and signed everyone to long-term contracts. This is an interesting example as ostensibly Infinity Ward was set up as an external developer, but from the start they were groomed purchase and becoming an internal studio for Activision. *Call of Duty* would have had to perform horribly for this relationship not to move forward and end the way it did. When founding my own studio, Activision set up a similar deal with myself, albeit at a smaller scale, but that's a story for another chapter. Blizzard, DICE, BioWare and most other "big" names you know in game makers are all wholly owned by publishers as internal studios, and most started as external and independent.

External developers

External developers (sometimes called third-party developers) are standalone teams and companies separate from publishers. These are independent entities that make games for themselves, self-publish, or even develop multiple games for different publishers at once. For every relationship the specifics and details are unique, with ownership and responsibilities dependent on what is needed and agreed upon. Gearbox Software, Avalanche Studios and Telltale Games are good examples of independent studios that work with different publishers. CD PROJEKT, Valve and a few others blur the line as independent developers that also publish their own titles, and sometimes other developer's games.

Publisher

Publishers are the people actually paying for the development of the game. Some publishers focus on a single platform such as console, PC or mobile, while larger publishers create dozens of games on all platforms. Activision, Electronic Arts, and SEGA are examples of these larger publishers often responsible for the marketing, PR, QA and many other aspects of game creation that surround but do not include developing the actual game. More details about these publishers are covered in later chapters.

That's about all you need to know for our journey through the games industry. We'll touch on other aspects as we encounter them.

The story so far: A VERY brief overview of games

I was at Microsoft's head office in Redmond, Washington, before the original Xbox was released in 2001. There was a meeting of game developers visiting the campus on how to release games for this new console. Microsoft had never done anything like this before and were looking to us for what we would like to see in a release process. It was also a good excuse for us to talk with other developers and see the latest versions of the games they were working on for the platform launch. None of this ended up memorable to me in the end— let me explain why.

We were on campus for these meetings and just breaking for lunch. Microsoft's campus is huge, but one of the main hubs of activity was the cafeteria. We headed there and ordered some decent looking food—I don't recall what exactly—but as we a place to sit down, our Microsoft handler nonchalantly pointed out "Oh look, it's Alexey Pajitnov.".

Now that name may mean nothing to you, but if you were ever swearing while waiting for that "long straight block" in Tetris... that's the man you should blame. Yes, that man personally accounted for hundreds of my gaming hours and is partly responsible for my career in making games. There he was, just sitting there, eating his lasagna. Noticing my rapt attention towards Mr. Pajitnov, we were asked, "Want to meet him?". *Um, yes!* We walked over and sat down at the same table and tried to look nonchalant. After a brief introduction, we started eating. He was quite pleasant but was just finishing, and it seemed odd to start bombarding him with questions, so we left him in peace. I am sure he does not even recall that day, let alone that meeting, but to me it was HUGE.

Before getting too deep into talking about the games industry, we need to get a general overview on both the history and current state to give some context about what the rest of the book will cover.

The games industry is $20+ billion a year in the US alone, with a worldwide estimate of $113 billion by 2018. There are other, more in-depth books that talk about the history of the industry but the key beats are listed below. Although mine are a bit bias to what I was playing or making at the time, I do think it hits the high points.

1) Late 1970s to mid-1980s: Atari, Coleco, PC gaming

2) Mid-1983: Games industry crash and the rise of Nintendo

3) Late 1990s: Rise of 3D gaming

4) Early 2000s: Console gaming returns strong and is back in full swing

5) 2008: Smartphones and mobile gaming takes off

6) 2010: Free-to-Play becomes mainstream

7) 2016: Year of VR

1) Origin of gaming at home 1977 (AKA Atari)

Gaming for me and most of the west mainly started with the Atari 2600. Affordable compared to a computer (which were not considered a home appliance yet... let alone entertainment), easy to use, and hooked up to any TV via a small switcher box that read "Game - TV", a quick flick of the black slider to "Game" had you playing *PAC-MAN* or *Defender* in seconds. Hugely successful for Atari and selling over 30 million units worldwide, this console created the market when home gaming didn't really exist before. Atari introduced the concept of joysticks at home and multiplayer gaming (on the same TV screen since there was no internet), becoming the pioneers of making gaming a mass market affair. There were other home gaming machines pre-Atari that only played one or two games. Although these consoles sold fairly well, they were seen as novelties and all but forgotten when someone saw an Atari 2600 in action.

2) 1983: the big crash and the rise of Nintendo

Before 1977 hip hop was barely known outside the Bronx, but the blackout in June of that year changed all that. DJs and artists who could not afford equipment took advantage of the outage, either looting the equipment directly or with other gains related to this opportunity bought equipment soon after the blackout ended. Hip hop not only changed its sound dramatically afterwards, expanding significantly as artists had access not only to the equipment but the explosion of talent within the industry from all the new artists creatively inspired from each other. This event helped solidify and expand the genre, ensuring its place in the music industry.

So what's this got to do with video games? We had something similar happen, a traumatic experience that I think paved the way for the games industry to be what it is today.

There are some great books and documentaries with varying opinions regarding what happened in the mid-1980s that caused the video game crash, but one thing they agree on is it happened and was devastating. Revenues went from $3.2 billion in 1983 to $100 million in 1985. Oversaturation of the market from different consoles, shoddy games, and competition from home PCs all contributed to the crash. It was very close to the end of gaming in the US, giving rise to Japan as the centre for gaming years to come.

The crash in 1983 brought games as an industry to its knees. The first ripple felt that should have been a warning sign was a huge increase in the number of games being made (a high proportion of terrible quality) with companies trying to make a profit with volume. This resulted in many, if not most game developers closing as that was an ill-conceived plan, a "hail Mary" attempt to shore up profits. Terrible quality is a gross understatement as companies literally threw out half done games that were poorly designed, terrible to play, and just plain awful. Some of the "worst games of all time" happened in this period such as Atari's *E.T. the Extra-Terrestrial*, which was one of the last straws for the industry. The result was a huge glut of games ending up in bargain bins at your local department store.

This meant that kids like me, who could not afford many games just a year or two before, could suddenly pick up ANY game for a dollar at the local Zellers, SAAN, or equivalent [1] store. I ended up

---

[1] Zellers and SAAN were Canadian chain department stores known for their inexpensiveness. Think Walmart, Target, and Kmart in the US.

owning pretty much every major Atari game. The result of the market crash led to the generation of ideas, cross-pollination of thoughts, and exposing the next generation of game makers to SO much more content than their predecessors.

The other benefit was the cleanse itself. Much like a forest fire is about renewal after the fact, all the dead underbrush and waste is cleared, allowing the ungerminated seeds a chance to start anew. Bad companies, ideas, and practices were swept away, and the next generation of game development began. The Japanese revolution and other future breakout success stories could not have happened without this opening created, and game makers like myself would not have an opportunity even 10 years later to enter the industry if this financial gaming apocalypse did not occur.

This brings us to Nintendo. In 1985 the Nintendo Entertainment System (or NES) was released in North America, changing everything and single-handedly saving the gaming industry. Characters such as Mario became household names, breaking out well beyond their games and entering into pop culture. Nintendo also introduced the concept of third-party development, authorising developers to produce and distribute titles for Nintendo's platform. This created a wide catalogue of high quality games on hardware well beyond what other systems could provide, including games unavailable for PC due to copyright or technological restrictions.

3) 1995: Rise of 3D gaming

This did not mean PC gaming stood still while all the exciting stuff was happening with consoles. By the mid-1990s, myself and others were making games while a new piece of hardware was coming out that would change the industry. The advent of 3D graphic cards for your PC provided proper 3D polygonal real time rendering, textures, and faster framerates in games that could not be matched by software renderers[2]. Games looked amazing from this hardware revolution which included a few hiccups and format wars. Once the dust had settled, PC gaming had transformed.

By the early 2000s, with the support of Microsoft and Direct 3D[3] accepted as the standard, PC graphic fidelity had pushed gaming on that platform to unparalleled heights. From that point on, consoles were playing catch-up to PCs for graphics since only updating their

---

[2] Rendering is when the computer "draws" anything on the screen. Hardware renderers are exponentially faster at doing this over software renderers that use the computer processor itself to do the job.

[3] Direct X and Direct 3D are libraries (or code) written by Microsoft that tells your computer how to render things acting as a unified language optimised for speed and quality.

hardware every 5+ years, while a newer and better video card was released every other month by one manufacturer or another. This is also where the "camps" formed in my opinion, the console gamers versus PC gamers. These camps refer to each other with derision nowadays—I'm still not sure why. This division is even more accentuated today if you just browse any gaming message board or discussion group online. PC Master Race is a "thing" that PC players flaunt while showing off their tweaked PCs and games as pinnacles of gaming. Some of these PC gamers go so far as stating console gamers are "not real gamers", which is silly as 80-90% of all non-mobile games sold in recent years are to console gamers.

4) 2000: Console gaming golden age

Nintendo did not remain alone for long in the console world. SEGA was their arch rival for years with the Master System, Genesis and host of other hardware that kept Nintendo on their toes. In 1994 Sony released the PlayStation which was a huge leap forward in technology, especially graphically for the console world. There were three big players now in the console wars: Nintendo, SEGA, and Sony. Who knew that in 2001 a company known for office software and " OS that was on everyone's PC" would enter the fray and contribute significantly to the demise of one leader in the console

20

war. On November 15, 2001, Microsoft released the Xbox. Despite the hardware and titles available for the launch, few thought it was a serious contender. Fast forward a few years, the available consoles are now Nintendo 64, PlayStation 2, and Xbox. SEGA's last console was the Dreamcast released in 1999, which sold poorly and discontinued by March 2001.

5) 2008 - Rise of mobile gaming

Apple was not really synonymous with gaming beyond the early days in the mid-1980s and the Apple II, but the company had a huge role in gaming's future. On January 9th, 2007, Apple announced entering the phone business market, and pretty much everyone laughed. Oh boy, were the critics wrong. Apple was not the first manufacturer of the "smartphone", but they were a major reason why smart phones are so popular today. More importantly Apple popularized "the slab" look: a big screen with nearly all controls located on the touchscreen. Essentially every phone afterwards followed this look, but more important than unifying user experience was the App Store. In 2008 Apple opened the App Store, and the gold rush for mobile gaming really took off. There had been games for mobile phones in the past, but the new power of the hardware allowed smartphones to become a real platform. Add an easy way to publish a game through the App Store, even a solo person with some skills could create and launch their very own games to millions of potential gamers. Within a few years even the big publishers were spending significant resources chasing smartphone gamers.

6) 2010: Free to Play, a new way to make games

The next change came via the smartphone gaming industry, the Free-to-Play system of payment. Back in the early days of gaming there were demos, which included a concept called Shareware: basically a game demo with only the first few levels or some other barrier to the full game that you could play indefinitely for free. If you liked the game and wanted the full thing, you could pay to unlock the remainder with a license key you could enter[4], and the rest of the game would then become playable. The early days of mobile gaming resembled this model but quickly morphed and became more nuanced. As with any system, there are good implementations and poor ones. Free-to-Play as a concept can range from getting the full game for free, requiring monetary purchases for additional cosmetics[5], actual power, and progression, with variation

---

[4] The key usually consisted of 16 letter and numbers uniquely generated for one use. There were many different configurations and schemes.

between territories. In Asia "pay-to-win" models are accepted by gamers and even thrive, while in the west any competitive game with even a whiff of these mechanics bring out anger in the most benign game's fans. It has even left the mobile gaming market and entered into the PC gaming. Massively Multiplayer Role Playing Games (MMORPGs)[6] and Multiplayer Online Battle Arenas (MOBAs)[7] were the first to experiment and adopt Free-to-Play as a concept, and has steadily started to enter most genres of PC games. It's a delicate balance trying to make enough money to actually pay for the creation of the game and having the barrier to entry low enough so as many people as possible will try. Free is the lowest barrier you can make, so I don't think this payment model is going away anytime soon.

7) 2016: VR Begins

---

[5] Cosmetics such as character skins, pets, and other unique ways to express yourself but did not necessarily impact gameplay.

[6] These games usually have huge servers where hundreds or thousands of people play online at the same time together, often with the other players being a key part of the gameplay. *World of Warcraft* and *EVE Online* are good examples.

[7] MOBAs are games where two teams face off online to destroy the other's bases, focusing on combat rather than unit construction or management unlike its real time strategy roots. Games such as *League of Legends* (LoL) and *Defense of the Ancients* (DotA) are good examples.

In 2015 a real buzz started around Virtual Reality (VR) and Augmented Reality (AR) as Oculus went from a crowdfunding "possibility" to a fully funded development when Facebook bought them for $2 billion. Is this the next shake-up in the gaming industry? At the time of this writing (March 2016), Facebook's Oculus Rift has started shipping, HTC VIVE is about to ship, Sony has their PS4 VR scheduled to launch in fall, and Microsoft HoloLens is shipping developer kits. From the developers I have worked with to speaking with Oculus and other VR manufacturers, both are spending serious money into the VR market. The technology seems to have caught up with the ambition. As a creator, this technology is every bit exciting as when 3D cards came out in the late 1990s, maybe more so. We have been imagining VR technology since 3D became possible: *creating* and *living* in a fully immersive world, and *being* part of the game beyond watching by fully and entirely embracing the suspension of disbelief. Most major game developers, publishers, and hardware manufacturers are betting this technology is the next step in not only gaming but how we consume content.

From gamer to game maker: What's life like working in games?

I was working at BioWare and moved into an apartment building across the back alley from the offices. We counted 32 footsteps. We also calculated the weather would have to be -70°C and a high windchill before forcing us to put on a jacket when going to work. This was a terrible thing as we discovered—the distance, not the weather, although Edmonton in the winter is hardly fun. We worked until the point of basically passing out at our desks. *Why not?* We did not have to drive home or even really walk. We could stumble back and forth between home and work so easily that there ceased being a difference between the two locations. Even during the weekends we came in a few times half-dressed in a bathrobe and slippers. This was not healthy. We led this "mole like" existence for far too long until moving a respectable ten minute walk to the office—our lives greatly improved.

Another BioWare example I remember was late 1996 or early 1997 while working hard on *Baldur's Gate*. BioWare's offices were located in a taller building on Whyte Avenue a trendy university area with more than its share of pubs and cheap restaurants in Edmonton, Alberta, Canada. We were a crew of 30 or so 18 to 24 year olds working their first job in the games industry. After 16 hour days we would go drinking in the evening, coming back to work for 9 or 10 a.m. the next day... and repeat. At 19 years old, you can work and party hard and never really sleep—I shudder even thinking about attempting that lifestyle now.

A key part of game development to understand is that during the early parts of the project there is not much to see: it's a lot of documentation, spreadsheets, and programmers working diligently behind-the-scenes to set up the code foundations and tools that form the base of the game being made. There is literally nothing to see in the game for months, except lines of code. Even when the very first pixels are rendered, the experience is always underwhelming. "Look, a grey box[1] that paths across the screen correctly!" is a HUGE victory, even if visually the accomplishment is "meh".

---

[1] Grey boxing is a term that refers to making temporary objects, testing elements without spending time to create actual high quality assets

One particular story about the importance of behind-the-scenes involves James Ohlen, lead designer on *Baldur's Gate*. Ohlen and his design team worked crazy hours to stay ahead of the artists and other programmers making sure people knew what to make next. These monumental efforts ensured games system design to dialogue and quest creation were available so content was ready for editors to start working. I started as a designer before becoming the Associate Producer, my responsibilities primarily tasking, reviews of the new content as it came in and generally greasing any wheels to ensure everyone on the team could do their jobs. This afforded me the opportunity to see every aspect of the game being made, including much of the "cool stuff" first.

During that week we were implementing a lot of new features , including some of the background art properly rendering in the 64 x 64 tiles and watching concepts come to life for the first time in the game. The last few weeks had seemed longer with the crunch time and deadlines so we ordered in some food. I was sitting in the artists' office while we ate, watching the most beautiful sunset through the large windows that covered one wall. . We all stood and ate in silence, bathing in orangish light as we faced the outside world and enjoyed. It was a nice quiet moment. I thought we should get James since he would appreciate it and needed a break anyway. I shouted down the hall "Hey James, come in here. There is an amazing sunset—you should see this!" I hear him come tearing down the hall, around the corner into the office and plonk down into one of the artist's chair. Hunched over and staring intently at the PC screen while completely oblivious we were staring out the windows with our backs to him. He asks "Where? Where?"

That's how far gone James was. "Hey look at this sunset" could *only* mean something about the game. Game developers tend to get wrapped up in their work. James was no better or worse at this than most—it's just a good example of someone loving what they do so much that the outside world tends to dim slightly. If not careful, developers be trapped within their own tunnel vision.

Years later in 2006, I was working with id Software and Splash Damage on *Enemy Territory: Quake Wars*. Kevin Cloud, one of the founders of id (located in Mesquite, Texas) and head honcho of art, was on one of his many visits to Splash Damage in England to review and sign off various milestones and discuss open design issues in the game. This meant Kevin Cloud, Paul Wedgewood (owner and creative lead at Splash Damage), and I were in a room with a PC, going over everything from map design, weapons, and vehicles to low level design issues such as specific weapon damage that were hot topics. This went on for hours as there were many items to cover and getting the three of us in a room together did not happen often as we'd prefer. It was approaching 10 p.m., we were still in the same boardroom, staring at old sandwiches from lunch ten hours ago that were soggy and unappetising while arguing over the colour that the Strogg (*Quake*'s main villain alien race) blood should be. It was a lively discussion.

"Green!"

"No.. Too stereotypical. How 'bout we make it more brownish green?"

"Like bile?" "Nah... Orange! It can be corrosive, and I am sure we could come up with a cool shader to really make it 'pop!'"

Back and forth we went on this important topic since this decision would be cannon for all future games in the *Quake* universe. And suddenly, we all stopped. We looked at each other and realised pretty much at the same time we have the best jobs in the world. Yes, we were tired, yes we were hungry, but we were spending our time debating what colour alien blood should be in our game. We were being PAID for this. We went with orange, in case you were wondering.

So what is it actually like to work in the games industry? Even as the industry continues to mature, there are times when the day-to-day work making games is just that—work. I love what I do, and in general the vast majority of the people I work with also love it. Currently in the industry, there is less "crunch" time (where you work much longer hours to meet deadlines), and when it does occur the time periods are shorter than when I first started. This is mostly due to better scheduling and organisation, but still some days are awfully long and development can go horribly wrong without warning with needing quick thinking and hard work to pull it out of the fire. I try to explain this to anyone considering entering the video game industry, especially as a developer. No, you do not sit all day "just playing games".

You also tend to lose perspective both inside and outside work. After the twentieth day in a row of late, pizza-fuelled nights, life tends to start getting fuzzy. In general, work/life balance is something that I have seen most people get wrong in the gaming industry. This is doubly for new or younger devs. When getting a dream job and loving what you do,, the world outside work like friends, family, and loved ones can get lost in the mix. Overall the industry has gotten better over the years and people are more aware of this "trap"; however, it is still a real issue since work and life can blur all too easily.

The games industry is unlike any 9-to-5 job that you may have experienced. Many if not most of the people that work in the industry are gamers that play as well as make games. This has a side effect where work and play start blending and differentiation becomes difficult. Another factor is that most people get involved quite young, so the concept of balancing life in a healthy way does not even register. "I am making games, this is great!" is pretty much the entire thought process. Working 14+ hour days and coming in on weekends to work (and play) more does not seem a problem when you have few outside attachments or commitments.

In the past there was even more pressure from both peers and the companies to work extra hours. In the mid-1990s until quite recently, it was looked down upon if you worked "normal" 9-to-5 hours. It would never show up on your employment reviews per se, but it was definitely noticed and unofficially taken into account when raises, promotions, and other aspects of your career were discussed. "Not going the extra mile" for the project was viewed as being less invested, which is insanity and plain unfair. It all started to change for me personally as I became older, got married, etc. When you have good reasons NOT to be at work, you start to question the 90 hour weeks you are putting into a project.

Another contributing factor was poor project management. Proper scheduling, tasking, and estimates for creating a game are rather difficult to create. Often developers create from nothing new features unseen in previous games. Twenty years ago nearly every part of the game was created from scratch, regardless whether other solutions were available. This approach was for perceived speed of integration into the rest of the project, but sometimes it was just pride. Reinventing the wheel over and over when unnecessary was a pitfall I saw trap many teams. Now that projects and project leaders are more experienced, a third party solution to a problem is definitely considered. From physics, sound, whole engines to minor items like fonts, off-the-shelf solutions are a timesaver, offloading some of the content and requiring fewer in-house features which makes the game easier to estimate. There are fewer dependencies and a host of other efficiencies that are gained and the additional expertise provides better estimates overall for a design, feature, or piece of content.

Lastly the whole scheduling system has matured overall. No longer shooting from the hip, experienced project managers are involved from the beginning with a work focus revolving around ensuring schedules are created, updated, and adhered. Making games as an industry has grown up a great deal and is treated like a business due to current big budgets, jumping from $1 million USD in the mid1990s to now over $200 million USD. With that amount of money spent requires accounting for time responsibly. Honestly this is both good and bad. We have gained much but lost some of the innocence and innovation that can't exist in this environment. This is part of the reason of the recent increase in the number of the indie and small scale development studios and projects, as well as why mobile game development has taken off as they typically exist outside this type of pressure.

The real turning point and first openly discussing industry issues was in 2004 by anonymous blog poster "EA Spouse" (later to be identified as Erin Hoffman). The blog focused on EA's practices of long hours that were not compensated for with overtime, and how it was basically expected that employees would accept the practice or be ostracised, or worse. EA by no means was unique in their behaviour—it was pretty much universal with not only the publishers but most developers. This led to class action suits against EA and changes to laws enabling overtime pay for certain positions that were slipping through the cracks through questionable definitions of who should qualify. Most importantly exposing this problem made it a topic of open discussion among people working in the games industry. After this incident, "good work-life balance" started showing up on company job descriptions and corporate pages. After this incident, the games industry started to "grow up" and is better off .

Even with these attitude shifts, people in the games industry still work long hours and take few vacations. Every year HR chases employees to spend their vacation time because they have days, weeks, or even months saved up. Common excuses are "There is just no good time to take time off". You are either planning, executing, or shipping a game, and any time lost seems critical. That's partially right. I have found there is never a good time, so just take it. Taking a vacation over the week you are actually shipping a game is probably not wise, but any other time would work. *You cannot predict what will happen, so don't put your life on hold because of "what ifs".* Even saying that, I'm just as guilty. I did not take a real vacation for the first 6 years I worked in games. Not because I wasn't allowed (BioWare was good at that overall), but I felt always needed and cared deeply about the games we were working on.

Another question I get asked often is "How much money do game makers make?"

This varies a huge deal, depending on not only the position and the amount of experience, but size of the company and your location.

Overall I have noticed a large number of unreasonable expectations from people just getting into the industry, either just finishing their education or working on their first game with a "real" company. I think this stems from the "old days" where profit sharing was more common which does not reflect the landscape of the industry today. Googling "average game industry salaries" displays a wide range. Someone starting out in QA for instance may be paid minimum wage as it's generally considered an entry level job. Generally programmers start at a higher salary and overall have a higher ceiling as they tend to have more education, but this is far from written in stone and salary may have as much to do with supply and demand.

Yes, you can live quite comfortably after a few years of paying your dues, just like any other professional industry with the top earning salaries in the hundred thousands dollars per year. Most of the people I know who have gotten rich in the industry started their own companies. Of course, most of the broke ones I know did the same.

Something that happens far less now than before is employees at a developer having shares in the profits of the game they are working on. This was often early in the life of a development studio to compensate for low wages and long working hours since they had little to no capital for paying employees properly. This can be a great if it works out or a terrible waste of months or years at the end for little to no benefit. Whether you want to take a job depends on your personal situation and if you can afford taking the risk.

Understanding the risk is key before taking a position, and if you are new to the industry, trust me, you don't understand everything that can makes a success or go wrong and needs mitigating. In my younger days starting out I would have considered joining these higher risk ventures, but now the "all or nothing" situations seem like a silly risk.

The last and honestly most rewarding part of making games is watching gamers enjoy playing them. I remember as a kid playing my first games on the Atari 2600 or old PC and the joy I felt. Finding your own games on the store shelf, being played online and lighting up message boards with people having a great time is the best feeling of accomplishment. When *Baldur's Gate* shipped in 1998, I went to our local PC shop and found the game on the shelf, proving to myself it was actually done. I witnessed a gamer excitedly grab one from the shelf and run to the counter. If I never shipped another game again this moment made it all worthwhile.

In over 20 years with 18+ games shipped, a million players have played the result of the hard work and dedication of teams I have been lucky enough to be a part of. It's even more rewarding when seeing those top "X" lists of games with a few of your titles And again, it is crazy how I have been so fortunate and honoured to work with so many great teams over the years.

Yes—bottom line working in the games industry is sometimes a slog like any other occupation, but it's the best job in the world.

A gamers "office": Where you are when you are not sleeping

BioWare, 1995/1996 in Edmonton Alberta Canada:

The company first started in a smallish, irregular office above a coffee/sandwich shop. We were located in the University area just off Whyte Avenue in Edmonton, Alberta (Canada). Between pizza located around the corner and that sandwich shop, our food was covered. The floors were uneven and creaky, and we had power issues. There were about a dozen of us in total with most of us bringing our own PCs to work. This was the very early days, and the company had not signed up our first full project with Interplay which would become *Baldur's Gate*. The carpets were ragged and did not cover the floor in places, and everything was marked up and stained, but we didn't care. The space was cheap (I assume) and served its purpose. Honestly it was only one step above where squatters lived.

There were five of us from a small town 600 km north of Edmonton that had been working on our own game. When we moved down, BioWare hired all of us at the same time, basically doubling the size of the company. During our first few days, we did not know how to act at all. We were 19, and never worked with others outside our group and had no idea what to expect. The founders of the company were medical doctors. Yes, they were fresh out of university themselves (hence our office location I suspected) most definitely gamers, and 26... old guys to us. When our original group previously worked together, the structure was far from organised, and we played games, swore, and in general acted like 19 year olds... *Is that ok? Is this a real job now? They are paying us to be here.*

During our initial meetings before being hired, we spoke mostly to the doctors and shared a few meals together, but we assumed everyone was a professional-like, serious grown-up. When we first arrived, BioWare artist Russ Rice welcomed us, but we did not know him very well. was already employed by BioWare. A little bit older than us, Russ wore bright, gaudy button up short sleeved shirts, ate the most incredibly unhealthy food, and was rail thin. He was our first introduction to a professional game maker.

Two minutes into our first day, Russ shouted out "FUCK!" to no one in particular at the office. I'm still not even sure why. He proceeded then to show us a website with the tagline "The pig-butt-nastiest place on the internet". *Whew, the rest of the employees were just like us.* The doctors (Ray, Greg and Aug) were absolutely just like us, gamers. Within a very short period of time, we felt at home, like a group of mates hanging out and trying to create something great. We were on a shoestring budget, but the camaraderie was very real and got us through. We ate together and drank together. What little time we were not working together was spent hanging out. Russ had a night job as a DJ at a dive bar a short walk away where we would hang out after hours where we spent entirely too much time drinking instead of sleeping. It was a fantastic introduction to the industry.

id Software mid-2000s in Mesquite, Texas

I had been playing id Software games since there were id Software games. My favourites included the first *DOOM* game, *Wolfenstein 3D*, and the *Quake* series in whatever incarnation. Fast forward a few years, I was working for Activision as a Producer/Creative Director on an id Software game, adding another checkmark on my list of things I wanted to do in the games industry before I died. Part of this goal was visiting id Software at their office in Mesquite, Texas. I had never been to Texas or to id Software, but the thought of visiting this sacred developer (in my mind anyway) overrode any silly hesitance about visiting a right-wing haven where my only reference points were stereotypes of guns everywhere and intolerance everywhere else (Texas BTW is an awesome place—I have rarely been surrounded by more friendly people).

This developer was famous for making games that took place in hell with demons and death as their trademarks. There was no surprise the office was in a dark depression at the side of a hill, with a foul odour perceptible long before you could even see the place... just kidding.

The office was in a business park and completely nondescript, as so many other developers. Not what I was expecting, but anyplace that brought hell literally to life should stand out a little bit, but id Software certainly did not. There were some expensive cars in the parking lot, but the office could easily been any tech company from the outside. Upon entering the building and wandering around trying to find their actual office (the building had a few tenants), we finally found a simple door that lead to reception. Who greeted us is not what you would expect at a developer that creates nightmares for a living: Miss Donna. She probably had many titles in her life, but "id Mom" is probably most appropriate. Imagine a middle-aged Texas woman, dressed casually and comfortably in "mom" clothes, showing the friendliest and most welcoming attitude that you can possibly imagine. Southern hospitality does not even begin to cover Miss Donna's charm. And I don't mean a forced smile for a company but a genuine warmth given to everyone she met. The entryway was simple, but the first sign we were somewhere special was a full, life-sized character from one of their games to the right of the main desk.

We got the grand tour before our meetings, which was very "normal" and not what I was expecting: long hallways with offices off to the sides, each housing several artists, programmers, and designers to a room. A central common/lunch room was stocked with coffee machines, snacks, and drinks with various levels of unhealthiness... but they did have fruit bowls, too.

Yes, there were posters, models of vehicles, pictures of monsters, and assortments of LEGO and Nerf, and of course the usual gamer paraphernalia,. In fact, I think id Software is a good example of an average developer office, entering the "professional" phase in a studio's lifespan, flavoured with the personalities of both their employees and game titles. The early days of crazy (like when id Software co-founder John Romero got locked into his office and his fellow co-founder John Carmack used an axe to batter the door down—yes that happened) and other "rock star" type behaviour was well behind them. The company had more or less settled down as most successful developers end up doing. The first few years is like a frat house, eventually moving to a more normalised "grown up" place. Publisher offices tend to be different.

Publisher offices in general

Publisher offices tend to be a more corporate affair overall. Publishers are the money men of the industry, so they often answer to shareholders and other people whose trust is important to maintain. Having millions or billions of dollars spent every year on games seems risky to the traditional business world without cut-off jean shorts wearing, barefoot, and scruffy looking people with scantily clad anime screensavers providing updates on how development is going. Even though publishers tend to be more serious, they still make games, so there is usually a meeting in the middle between business and casual.

A look at Activision in the early 2000s

Activision's Santa Monica offices are located in a business park a few miles inland from the beach. The outside is pretty nondescript with a coffee shop and chain restaurant (I recommend the Moroccan mint or jasmine tea with honey and the clubhouse sandwich respectively) sharing the same direct parking lot with a big blue "Activision" sign hanging on the front.

The front entrance (if you have a keycard or get "buzzed in") is a fairly standard desk with reception, awards, and other promotional posters, standees, and life-sized models of various characters scattered around. These displays change based on which games are on the market or what is being promoted at the time.

Quality Assurance (QA) is located in the basement with the headcount ebbing and flowing depending on when games are shipping. The summers are the busiest with many temporary staff filling the ranks. Many titles will be tested at once on every piece of hardware that can play games from PCs to consoles. One large room of cubes, hardware is scattered everywhere with a few offices in the very centre where the managers sit. QA staff are probably the closest in appearance to the stereotypical game developers. I have talked to surfers, bikers, metal heads, university students, geeks, and one guy I could of sworn was Amish down in QA. The one universal thing is that they are young and enthusiastic gamers coming from all walks of life.

The ground floor was mostly corporate, accounting, and legal, and where most of the upper management offices were located. I did not spend much time on the floor during my workdays, but in general this was the most "normal" office area with lots of calendars on walls and meeting rooms. This area was where most "outsiders" ended up when visiting. It was also where playing games was not a requirement to do the job. An accountant needs to be passionate about numbers and order, not worrying about which perks to take in the latest *Call of Duty* game; however, the great majority of anyone who works at a publisher are gamers, even in these departments.

The next floor up is where Activision development started. This was back in the early 2000s, is where much of the dev was still happening inside Activision head office. The layout of the offices, no matter what floor, was an "8", basically two squares. The outside of the "8" had offices and the middle lined with cubicles. The flow and layout changed over time, but the design, decoration, and personalisation on the first floor was much like any other developer studio whether inside a publisher's walls or not.

The third floor is where I spent most of my time which was a mix of third-party publishing supporting a developer not owned by Activision but the game was being published by the company, and more in-house development. One section was console development, and our side was "shooters". We called it 4710 as that was the cost code for the department accounting (creative I know), and we worked on games from id Software, Raven, Infinity Ward, etc.

Offices and cubes were littered with posters from games, TV shows, and movies. Transformers, LEGO, Nerf guns and any other "geek toy" imagined was on display somewhere on the floor. There were limits, however. In a bigger company with an official Human Resources (HR) department, the realms of taste are maintained. They were not unreasonable, but there was a corporate "feel" that didn't exist at a developer. Maybe it was the fact we were closer to the money being spent, and the day-to-day was not purely creative. Maybe it was because the investors, president, or CEO of this multibillion dollar company could walk down the hall at any moment, and if they hesitated about the security of their investment, bad things could happen.

In summary, game making offices both in development and publishing look like most other offices but with basically more toys and swearing.

Production: The "behind-the-scenes" of behind-the-scenes people

My first publisher producer job was with Activision in 2001 on *Soldier of Fortune II*. Now I had the chance to see publishing from the other side of the fence instead of as a developer, working far more deeply with Marketing, PR, and QA, and the other, seemingly more unfathomable aspects of game making. I had an executive producer above me and several associate producers reporting to me. We worked as a team, dividing the workload usually based on experience, but sometimes just on preference or seniority for the fun stuff. At first glance this role was similar to being a development producer at BioWare and Relic Entertainment, I added working on P&L (profit and loss) sheets, green-light meetings, product pitches, and design reviews, because of my developer background, to my growing list of responsibilities. I discovered as a publisher producer you normally have very little access to the low level aspects of the game beyond milestone review feedback. Personally I felt too far removed from the actual game making for my own taste. Once you reach or rise above the title of Senior Producer within most publishers, the role worries far more about budgets, schedules, and the health of the project within the company rather than the actual game. This role is exceedingly necessary, especially in a AAA game, but did not match my personal preference as a career path. Due to my own strengths and preferences, and the incredible insight by my own managers (which I'm grateful for), I mainly worked on projects that required more of a "design hat", providing extra help to the teams that focused the overall direction of the game. I ended up onsite at the developers for months, or even years, at a time as a creative lead, while still technically serving as a producer. Yes, I worried about milestones and still dealt with marketing and PR, but much of the rest of my production roll was taken on by other publisher producers so I could focus on the day-to-day with the team.

Things have changed a lot since I first started making games professionally in the mid-1990s. Teams and budgets were a tenth the size as they are today, and the scope and scale of the games were greatly reduced to match. In those early years, organization was relaxed, which is a kind way to say it. Schedules rarely went beyond a straight task list, maybe Post-it Notes on a board somewhere when dependencies[1] were involved. Coordinating a dozen people could be managed by a single person fairly easily, and many other aspects of the project fell to this position as the *Producer*.

But what kind of producer? Producer at a developer or publisher? What's the difference? I have discovered over the years that the term is near to useless in actually describing a position or even a set of skills. The only constant is that "a producer enables his team to create a game". A good producer delivers on time and budget. A great producer accomplishes all that and everyone is happy, but the challenge being every company is different and every team has different requirements. The best overview I can show is examples of producer roles I encountered over the years

My first actual production job was at BioWare on the *Baldur's Gate* series in 1996. Scheduling, uploading builds, working with localisation, and being the contact point for Marketing, PR, and press tours while managing the personalities on the team were aspects of my day-to-day. Acting as the conduit between BioWare and my Interplay producer counterparts was a main focus, and ensuring milestones were reviewed and approved was pivotal. I was

---

[1] Dependencies are tasks that require previous tasks to be done first. You must build the fence before you can paint it.

a development producer—if an issue wasn't art, design, or programming, it was production (AKA everything else). Eventually the team became big enough that we started getting more assistant and associate producers to help with the sheer amount of grunt work needed to make the game.

In 2009 I was hired as a creative consultant for EAP[2] to work on *Crysis 2* among other project. EAP had broken down the producer role into all the elements catering to the specialties that people focused on. The development director's key focus is scheduling and navigating EA's different departments to get what the team needed. Other production roles included art director, creative director, tech director, and more traditional production roles. All were considered producers, but because of the scope the game could never be covered by one title or person. This approach is the most logical and sensible breakdown I have seen so far except the titles are often misleading because of the desire (or lack of new terminology) to keep the "producer" name. I first heard of this structure maybe ten years before and thought EA was crazy. How many producers do they need on a project? This was during my time wearing many "hats" as

---

[2] Electronic Arts Partners

a producer at Activision. After experiencing this approach first-hand, I now understand how specialisation leads to far higher quality work. "All-rounders" do many tasks well but not any one thing at a world class level compared to a specialist.

So what does this mean? In short, the role of producer shifts dramatically depending on where you are, the team's needs, and whether you are working for a developer or a publisher. It is the least descriptive job title in the industry, and for something that is so core to creating a game, we should come up with something better.

This is a breakdown of general production role

Publisher Producer

The scope of tasks ranges far more for a publisher producer than a developer producer since the role interacts with more people that know very little about the game. This producer has to communicate well, and have the ability to understand the needs and worries of these disparate groups to help solve any issues that occur. You are the buffer, the filter, and arbiter of the "crazy" that can sometimes surface from these groups, and responsible to ensure that the development team gets what they need for making the best game possible. These groups the Publisher Producer interacts with on a day-to-day basis vary in roles and responsibilities:

Developer: You are the main point of contact for the developer. If they need something, you are the one they call day or night. You are their "fixer"—from getting a replacement video card at a tradeshow, chasing a milestone payment, to checking up on an asset for a marketing video, you are the one ultimately on the hook to sort it out.

Marketing/PR: Throughout the project the marketing team, along with their marketing plan, will have requests for assets, articles, and support from the dev team for tradeshows and other promotional opportunities. No matter how well planned, there are always changes and last minute additions, and being able to support marketing without negatively impacting the development team is key.

Upper management: Video games cost millions of dollars to make, and it is only fair that upper management at publishers want some insight into how development is going. Whether it is some sort of "green-light" process, playtests, or presentations, the expectation is that many times through the game development the Publisher Producer will have to hold a "dog and pony show" and update people not directly on the project. A large part of the job is to straddle informing people on progress while getting them excited about the game. Losing confidence from any of these people can sink the game, but at the same time you need to be upfront with the challenges. It can be quite the dance.

Milestones: Development budgets are often broken down over milestones where the developer delivers a set of features and assets that are reviewed, and if everything is as it should be, they get paid. As a publisher producer a primary responsibility is understanding the schedule and signing off on the milestones. There can be a lot of pressure as a missed or unpaid milestone can ruin a developer, but at the same time paying because you like them isn't a good practice since a missed milestone is often indicative of a problem. It is the Publisher Producer's job to identify and sort out the problem.

Third-party software/partners: Most games incorporate other technology or assets from third-parties from physics engines, user interface (UI) technology, to assets from outsourced groups. The Producer Publisher is in the middle, making sure there are contract and sign-off requirements.

First-party publishing partners: Managing relationships with companies like Microsoft and Sony, including paperwork at the concept stage of a game to working and negotiating bugs/QA sign-off at the end of the process before going to manufacturing

Quality assurance: Starting at Alpha version, your game enters into QA where bugs and issues are highlighted then entered into a database. As the contact point for many aspects of these bugs, the Producer Publisher helps to triage, close, or even fix some of these issues.

Localization: Games are not just in English and require translation into 12+ languages before shipping around the world. The coordination of localized assets, builds of the game[3], and testing go through production.

Other duties (aka "the rest"): Getting games rated for release (e.g. Teen, Mature, etc.), setting up and running focus groups, coordinating tradeshows, running press tours, and much, *much* more.

Developer Producer

Publisher: The flipside to the publisher producer, the Developer Producer is in constant contact with the publisher of the game. Whenever the publisher has a question or a request, the Developer Producer answers questions about schedules, builds, assets, milestones, QA, and about anything else that funnels first through this role. You are the filter, the delegator, and first line of defence for anything that comes from outside the developer.

---

[3] A build of a game is a snapshot, fully functioning of the game so far. It is self contained and representative of the game at that moment.

Project leads: Responsible for coordinating the entire team, the first and main points of contact are the team leads. This role works closely with the lead artist/art director, lead designer/creative director, and lead programmer/tech director, and depending upon them to not only run their respective teams but constantly inform what is happening. In return, the Developer Producer is responsibility for solving their problems and conflicts, and keeping the team leads informed on any other aspect of the game they do not have direct contact.

QA: Most AAA games now have onsite QA that starts long before Alpha and is separate from the publisher QA. This onsite testing has a lead but coordinates with the rest of the development team via the producer. The testing starts early with the first playable code or prototype, and will run alongside development until reaching Alpha where responsibilities are split with the publisher QA. In general onsite QA has a much tighter "loop" with development due to close physical proximity, so they tend to test builds before sending to the publisher or specific features that the programmers and designers are currently working on. All of this needs coordination from the producer.

Upper management: Much like the publisher producer has pressure from upper management because of the money spent, the development producer has the same pressure from their own superiors. Even if the developer only has one project, the person running the company is often too busy to get involved with the day-to-day of the project and needs to be updated regularly. This communication is important when trying to ensure teams are properly resourced and schedules are adhered so that commitments can be delivered.

These descriptions are just for the "traditional" publisher/development relationship on an AAA title. Every company and game is completely different, and the scale and scope of both the team and the game will change the responsibilities greatly.

This huge amount of scope allows the producer to see and be involved in almost every part of the game unlike any other position. It is stressful since most often the role entails firefighting emergencies on the frontline regardless whose "fault" it is—it is the producer's problem to solve.

Programming is magic - ask any programmer

During 2015, I was in Russia visiting Artplant's programming and art team which are located in Tver, a decent sized city roughly three hours northwest of Moscow. I say three hours, but Russian roads in February make it unpredictable, mostly due to Moscow rush hour traffic, which is the worst in the world that I have seen (take that LA!). Tver is an ideal place to set up a programming team since several polytechnic universities are in the area, and in the town of roughly 500,000 there are so many people with engineering degrees that your local waiter probably has one. Another thing about Russian programmers is that they are seriously talented—scarily so much so that I refer them as "magical Russians"

We had been there for a day, and just before lunch I was talking to Igor (Russians pronounce it "eye gore" to my surprise), the tools programmer, about the latest version of the map editor for the game we were working on. I was one of many employees that used the program nearly every day, and we were casually talking about "quality of life " features that would make creating maps in our game easier. There is a minor language barrier if you go outside Moscow where learning English is not really a priority, but as we chatted back and forth he kept on nodding as I described my workflow. I did not know how much of it made sense to him as I spoke no Russian, and although Artplant programmers can type fluent English (we primarily talked online via Skype text) spoken/conversational English was a struggle sometimes, and I worried my own poor communication skills were going to confuse things worse.

I had to run off to lunch and meet with a few other people. When I returned, I was going to talk to Viv (Artplant's Project Manager) about setting up a more formal meeting to hash out what time we could cull for enabling Igor and I to work out and implement the features. I caught up with a few Artplant programmers at the quaint pub restaurant while enjoying an amazing Borscht—I hate beets but decided to try the soup at least once while in Russia and was so glad I did.

Upon my return to the office, Igor motioned me over and in broken English basically asked " Like this?". I sat down at his desk and on his screen was the editor but with *every* single feature I talked about implemented, almost exactly as I described over the time it took for lunch... If I was working with a US or UK team this process would have taken days to meet and plan followed by more days to implement I am sure... not for the magical Russians, however.

Programmers are key to game development, starting from the beginning to fixing any issues that happen at the end.

About Programmers

I am not a programmer—the last time I wrote any code was over 20 years ago; however, I keep on top of what is happening in the broad sense in order to do my job. Over the years I have learned the architecture basics in multiplayer systems, what a deferred render[1] is, and a whole host of specifics on how certain engines work. These basics continually impact practices in the industry, and having an understanding is useful for someone looking to join the industry as a programmer or new to the game making business and wants a better understanding of what goes into programming. More importantly, I

---

[1] Also, the term is sometimes called deferred shading. When the computer draws something on the screen, the process is done in several "passes", not all at once. Think of it like placing layers but faster than the eye can see so it appears simultaneous. Traditionally, before deferred renderers the shading was done at the same time as geometry was "placed" in the world. What this new technique does is let the geometry be placed on the first pass and apply the shaders on the second pass. This allows far less computing used for lighting, allowing the scene to use more lighting sources for far less resources.

have worked with some brilliant engineers in varying positions (depending on the company, people responsible for programming are called programmers, coders, or engineers).

"Types" of programmers - the R&D vs implementers

Over the years, I have noticed a trend in personality types and interests, and how they flow into two separate groups of programmers. Not all companies have the space to accommodate this bifurcation of talent but happens enough to mention. The programmers who write "white papers" that are shared among academia have often recently worked at a university or some research company. Everyone falling into this category are exceedingly specialised and usually near the top of their field of study, usually working on a new rendering technique for the next engine or network layer that deals with asynchronous latency[2] and competitive play. The R&D programmers generally do not work on code that will see the light of day in itself but come up with the concepts, designs, and technical architecture that enables others to

---

[2] Asynchronous latency refers to the time delay between two computers that are "talking" to each other online, but are not doing it in turns, or even waiting to hear back from the other computer before "talking" some more.

make these ideas and code relevant to the project. They can work alone but often as part of teams, and serve as the backbone for technical innovation in games. Every "neat" feature you have seen, from that cool cloth effect on your character's clothes to the awesome way your car crumpled when it hit that wall, all started with a very smart person researching some sort of pet project. Don't get me wrong, these programmers are not all unsung hero hermit-types.

John Carmack is a prime example of a coder who makes "cool things", which are then taken and made into games. If you have ever played a first person shooter , you can thank at least some part of that experience to John Carmack. In the developer id Software offices, there is no doubt in anyone's mind who the company and gaming revolved around. My last time there was about ten years ago when 120+ people working very hard on several projects. If John came out and said, "Hey, we should look at this", people would drop what they were doing and take a peek. Not everything he did was ground breaking, and he very rarely dealt with a project directly, but without him first person shooter (FPS) gaming would be very different if it existed at all.

The second type of programmer is the team member. He/she is at the core of the development team. Depending on the scope of the project, the number of programmers range from a small handful to huge teams with subteams of specialists working together on the game. These are the people that get things done as tools programmers, network engineers, or any other specialist. allowing everyone else on the team to complete their work. Artists, designers, and even other programmers are all "downstream" from them— without this critical work, nothing would ever ship.

One theme keeps coming up no matter what area of programming someone plans to specialise in— know your math. The number one lament I keep hearing from tech directors and lead programmers is that not enough programmers have a strong math background which is required for any area of competent coding.

Learn what you enjoy and specialize

On big titles there can be dozens of programmers working together to create a AAA game, but they don't just dogpile onto the task list and go crazy. Most programmers have a specialization in a particular area of programming. Each feature needs to be world class, and the scope and scale of the games in combination with the complexity and speed in which technology changes, no one person can be an expert in all aspects of programming. Some specific areas that programmers tend to focus on:

- Networking
- Graphics/rendering
- Artificial Intelligence (A.I.)
- Tools development
- Gameplay (a catchall but generally interacts with designers a great deal more)
- Engine (again a catchall but may involve a separate team not attached to a "game")
- Effects
- Animation
- Audio

By taking any game apart and describing its components, you find separate fields to specialize in. The larger the team, the more they tend to specialise. On the flipside, programmers part of a very small project or team will most likely need to be on top of multiple areas, but the scope and scale will be greatly reduced as well.

Pick your language/engine:

There are many languages to choose from, and over the years things shift slowly depending on the needs of the industry. There is no point learning and mastering Java or a HTML scripting language for making console games—instead become competent in C+C++ and C# before approaching a developer, and again include any demos, mods, and programming examples to prove your knowledge. Using engines such as Unity allow for the creation of a whole project, or even a game, with one- or two-person programming teams in a fairly short time period. Programming is much about mindset as it is about the language, and with diligence a programming language can be learned quickly.

Almost all developers use tests during the interview process, requiring that the programmer work out coding problems to prove their fluency. Tied into this exam is learning the context in which the code will be presented and understanding the engine. Whether Unity, id Tech, Unreal, CryENGINE, or one of the many others available, every engine has free access for playing and experimenting with, developing skills, and building knowledge. Every gaming engine has online support through active and helpful communities, places where discussions and posting questions can provide aid when a programmer is stuck or trying something new.

Other programming hints and tips

- Comment your code: Programmers do not work alone on a project, and the odds are that one day someone else will have to fix or add to this code. If the original programmer is not around or busy, stepping through every single line of code to figure out what is going on becomes a huge time sink. A few basic comments at the top of relevant sections can help a great deal. Don't think this ends with helping others. This programmer will be the first stop for fixing areas that they coded; 12 months later who knows how many features they've created are now required to review and remember the implementation of every single bit of code.

- Formatting and naming consistency: Most places will have a code review process including a format and standard practices for how to code. This is not just the programmer equivalent of a grammar Nazi. With dozens of programmers diving in and out of code over the course of a project, plus long term support and reuse of code, if it is not all uniform then deciphering becomes more difficult when everyone has their own "way".

- Reviewing and committing code: It sounds simple— review code before committing. As part of a team, committing code that breaks the build because a programmer could not be bothered to check their own work will not be on the team for long. The number of times a playtest or a review could not happen because of careless code commits should be approaching zero. Testing code before committing can avoid this issue altogether.

- Stay up to date, read whitepapers: The whole games industry moves at an incredible pace, and no place more so than programming. New techniques, technologies, and concepts evolve pretty much constantly. White papers serve as technical documents released to the public or select groups, and are released everyday sharing the latest ideas and concepts. There are conferences that happens several times throughout the year, which publish many if not all of the notes, attended by talented and forward-thinking people more than willing to share. Any programmer needs to stay on top of these.

The tech director or lead programmer is one of the most important, if not the most important, member of the team when factoring the quality of the game. No matter how great the design is or how talented the artists are, if the programming team cannot support the features or make the game run well on a platform, the effort is all moot. Many companies know this but take it too far. id Software is a "tech led" company, creating some great piece of technology and building a game around it. Other "tech led" companies include Crytek and their *Crysis* franchise, and even mobile games with NaturalMotion in the UK. These examples are companies that have succeeded in this approach for the most part. There is a risk, however, when making games this way—programmers love solving and creating technical challenges but not necessarily making fun games. The result may be a visual or technical marvel that is not fun to play. I am a firm believer that design should lead the way but needs to be in conjunction with the programming and art leads. If any one of the three disciplines are overrepresented in the process, this creates a serious risk regarding quality of the game.

Before centring a game around a piece of tech, developers must ensure they can answer the question "Why?". A game must deserve to exist. Having features for the sake of features is a foolish way to create a game. If the tech cannot be justified, instead of not pursuing, it may be better as a tech demo or white paper shared with others, or spending more time figuring out what gameplay and design can be gleaned. I have seen too many technical marvels pushed out to the public and then fall flat because they are not fun and could not answer the question "Why?".

My favourite type of programmer that I get to deal with in my day-to-day are the gameplay programmers. These are the men and women who work most directly with the game's designers and

Creative Director. They work primarily on the actual game and not the backend or core systems that make the game function, but the layer on top which describes the game. If there is a rule for a game mode in a first-person shooter, that's the gameplay programmer's job to implement. If you are making a weapon or reward for a player, that's the gameplay programmer again. The reason I like working with these people is they are almost always gamers and required to have a good design sense to do their jobs well. They go beyond reading from a document to implement a feature by interpreting the request and then implementing while keeping in mind all the restrictions of the engine or code. This means I end up having tons of conversations with them about "What if we do things 'X' way instead of 'Y'?" followed by "We can't do it 'X' because it will chew up too much memory and won't work". Solving gameplay problems through a technical lens is a whole other layer of problems-solving, and I find it extremely rewarding when a seemingly impossible problem is sorted through creative compromises and approaches. I enjoy talking to clever people who love games, and this area of programming tends to draw those types of people into the role.

Game Design: Who comes up with this "stuff"?

Lionhead in 2004 was working on a movie studio simulation called appropriately *The Movies*. I was working for Activision as the Creative Director/Producer and onsite at Lionhead full-time, enough so that my desk at Activision UK was a place for others to store "stuff". When I did return to the Activision UK offices, the receptionist totally did not recognise me and asked "So who are you here to see?". I actually had a hard time on more than one occasion convincing her that I worked there. I guess when pointing to my disused desk teetering with old hardware, spare video cards, and the office biscuits and fruit being shared that day did not make my argument more believable. Being away long-term onsite at developers actually got the nickname of "being on a Smedders" (*thanks James... sigh*).

My job was more or less being a "Peter Molyneux whisperer"—taking his high level design and working with people like Creative

Director Gary Carr to make into a low level design that a programmer or artist could use for implementing. Peter operates on another level, and he actually thinks differently from you or I. This is both good and bad. This type of thinking is absolutely fantastic if you want to do something new or push a boundary but can be rubbish when you just want to solve something simple, that does not need reinvention. He would also get bursts of inspiration from... well, just about anything really and want to change, add, and improve. He always did it from a good place and wanted to make something special... every time. Makes people like producers who want to schedule or ship games want to bang their heads against the wall, but from a creative point of view it's awesome.

There are other upsides to the way Peter works. He approaches problems from new angles. We were stuck with a design problem a few months from alpha where we were trying to come up with a method to teach the player some of the deeper aspects of the game but not in an overtly "tutorial way". The game itself was a cross between *The Sims* and a *Tychoon* game, and having pop-ups during gameplay seemed brute force and inelegant. We were in a meeting brainstorming, and Peter walks in and asked, "So what are you guys working on?" (Peter was rarely involved in the day-to-day of the project), so we explained the issue. He said, "What if you have advisors for the different aspects of the game just walk up to you?" You know, like any business you hire the accountant, the business managers, etc. They can be real people in the game and they could just 'do their job' and 'advise you'.".

What a perfect "in universe" way to solve the problem. He delivered the solution in such a casual and "off-the-cuff" way and just walked out in a "BOOM—problem solved! My work here is done…" kind of way. Now we had to design the entire system and figure out how it would work, but that silver bullet was very "Molyneux".

Philosophy

I have met a wide range of talented designers and designed my fair share of games and systems as well, and the process boils down to this:

"A good designer knows how to come up and implement a good game."

Sounds simple, but this statement goes very deep. The key is the "and implement" part of the statement. In order to succeed, the designer must understand all aspects of the game, tools, and technology involved. Coming up with a good idea is easy, anyone can quite honestly but being able to translate that idea into a working, playable, and *fun* game is where the real talent lies. Game design is a combination of knowing the limits, being ambitious, and pushing features while working within technical restrictions. I have met a many designers effective at game design, and if you want to be successful there are a few key practices needed .

Know your target audience and market.

This generally means understanding the type of game being made. I know the common misconception that people in the games industry have is "play games" all day and magically at the end a game is created, but in this case game playing is pretty much a requirement. Designers need to know what other developers are doing, extrapolate where things are going next, and get ahead of that. When sitting down to design a game, designers are not making it for competing against games available now but what *will* be out a year or two in the future. If creating a game comparable to the best offered today, the designer has already missed the mark, and the genre will have moved on by the time the game is released.

Have the 1,000 foot view.

Designers must "zoom out" and see each feature as a part of the whole. Does it fit? Does it add to the overall experience trying to be created? All aspects should be complimentary to what the designer is trying to achieve, and this can become esoteric and subjective.

A great man once said, "Collaborate and listen"[1], which is sage advice. Working as part of a team is key, and a good team is great but realize you are often not the smartest person in the room. Matter of fact, assume not. I personally prefer to come up with a feature, flesh it out, and pitch it to the other designers and have them kick it around. Find the holes, propose counter ideas. Never have an idea so dear that you are unwilling to hear criticism. Leaders lead their teams to the answers, they don't dictate wisdom from on high. Yes, a Creative Director needs to steer the conversations and features to keep development pointing in the right direction, but they do not single-handedly solve issues a vacuum. Some teams need more direction than others, but in the best approach is working in a collaborative fashion. Multiple smart people working together will always come up with a better answer than an individual.

One giant caveat—collaborative work does not absolve responsibility. Calls must be made, people must be held accountable, and features must be assigned and created. Having design by a cabal

---

[1] It's rapper Vanilla Ice. What? Vanilla Ice is a great man!

or committee is taking this concept too far, inviting only disaster. Striving for consensus on every decision is the rocket sled to mediocrity at best, and at worst being paralysed in arguments and stagnating progress.

"Stick to the core features and tenets of their design."

When starting a project, have a handful of tenets for describing and understanding the game. Each feature when pitched needs to fall into specific categories (I refer to them to as pillars) or should be cut. Possible pillars for a game:

- Science fiction
- Free running
- Skill-based shooter
- Deep character progression

When someone wants to add a progression system that revolves around maintaining a player base (the amount of players actually playing your game at any one time) the team is reaching too far when the foundations of the design does not support that feature. Even if it is the best base/progression system ever built, it falls outside the core features and should not be added. What elements can be brought into the pillars' scope? What makes the proposed feature cool and can then become relevant for the game? Adding a strong feature is not always a bad idea but realize the additional risk and scope change. Many projects have died in development due to the weight of "great ideas" piled on top of each other. Focusing and delivering on four or five core features is better than not delivering any of the envisioned features and failing on 20 fronts. Being focused in your design and making sure a feature fits securely within your well defined pillars is the simplest way to ensure a tight and cohesive game. More importantly you guarantee your time is spent exactly where it should be during development.

Understand the technical limitations.

A lesson best learned early with game design is realizing dreaming up amazing ideas is easy, but if the tech cannot support the idea, it is irrelevant. Involving the Tech Director or Lead Programmer during the creation of a core design feature is necessary to avoid serious development problems. The lead programmer is responsible for implementing every feature of the game, the technical design, and the tasking of each programmer. New features or concepts must be run by him/her first. Most ideas when broken down are simple to solve—it's the time required to code that matters more. Some features sound very simple but require whole new systems that could take weeks or months to implement. More experienced designers have learned to recognize these pitfalls, and either design around or understand the scope and curb other features before running into development roadblocks months into production.

"Keep it simple."

If a feature seems confusing to a player, the solution is to cut and not add. This is a pitfall that a lot of people, including myself, have fallen into. If a feature is not clear to the player the first instinct is to add helper notifications, systems to point out different facets, guide features to train the player to perform a desired behaviour… *Stop, just stop.* The problem is that the feature is too complicated or subtle First assess whether the feature is critical to the core game. If critical, a failure happened at the prototype stage which can be solved at the cost of time. If it is not core to gameplay, is it necessary? What does it add? Can aspects of the feature be automated? Make it more passive and still get the desired behaviour or results? And lastly, what are you trying to achieve and can it be done another way? In general, a game targeted towards a broader audience needs an easier learning curve, and the weak points clearly identified, and the extra clutter removed whenever possible.

Know when to cut a feature.

By sticking to the core tenants, solving confusion with efficient culling, working collaboratively within a team, your feature list becomes relatively accurate, doable, and reasonable; however, there are times when schedules change, estimates are wrong, features don't work in practice as on paper, and tough calls must be made. Refer to the above items to help you make those calls and be willing to cut scope until it actually hurts the core tenants. Then you must fight for the feature, which is a topic we will discuss later.

Be flexible, it's not always a straight path.

When I started at BioWare, I had never shipped a game before. In fact, no one at BioWare had ever shipped anything before. Although this inexperience has some obvious inherent flaws, it does have some significant upsides. We have absolutely no preconceptions of what or more importantly, what cannot be done. The original design for *Baldur's Gate* was insanely ambitious, but we were too ignorant to know implementing every feature would be impossible, so we did it. If someone right now gave me the scope for *Baldur's Gate* and said, "Ya, so this crazy scope, with tech that is being invented as they go along, with a team whose average age is maybe 21. And no one, not a single one of them, have shipped anything before", I would not even consider green lighting it. Old cynical me would pass on something inexperienced me never even considered a problem, which means on some level I have lost something. Interplay, who was our publishing partner and funded the development, was possibly crazy like us. More likely they noticed we were a small Canadian start-up, thought we were cheap enough that the risk was worth it, or didn't fully understand what we were proposing. In either case, I along with many others are very happy they decided to take the leap with us.

I remember my first task at BioWare, Day 1, 9:00 a.m. Ray Muzyka, one of the owners, sat me down and said, "Design the A.I. for the game". I was a university dropout thinking about taking law and had designed my own game with a small group of people but never got past the prototype phase. At first, I literally had no idea where to start. Was Ray crazy for thinking I could start with this? Long after, I realised giving me this challenge as the first task was a touch of genius. How do you design AI? Well you first need to understand the abilities of the NPCs (Non-Playing Characters), including the combat system, spell system, dialogue system, etc. At this point, the game did not exist, and we had not even tackled the major task of converting the turned-based rules of *Advanced Dungeons & Dragons* (*AD&D*) and making it "real-time" for the game. This task forced me to create an outline for the design of the whole game. The AI was basically the last task in that chain, and by dissecting what was needed, I could reverse engineer practically the entire *Baldur's Gate* game. The framework for the design documents all started from this single task of "design the AI". The actual design of the AI was done by a much smarter person, a programmer, but was based on the now supporting game design that was the template.

Even though I go far to discourage the false notion that people in the games industry just play games all day long, there is a nugget of truth in that assumption. Not all game design comes from thinking deep thoughts in a room full of smart people—sometimes even key features that you could never even imagine a game without are there only because of odd accidents or exposure to new things. The intelligence and skill comes in when the team needs to know when to seize these influences or accidents and incorporate them into the game.

New Years 1996/1997

Blizzard released the hit game *Diablo*, and it was a breath of fresh air into the action/RPG genre. Nearly all of us at BioWare were huge fans of Blizzard, and we quickly became addicts of their new game. I was the Associate Producer at the time for *Baldur's Gate*, and part of my job was to check tasks, make sure people were on schedule, dependencies delivered on time, etc.. At first, we played *Diablo* after work, late into the night, or at lunch. No one's work was really being affected, but after a few days I started seeing it on more and more screens during work hours. If people got their work done, who cares? Except playing the game instead of working was becoming a worry, and I knew it was just a matter of time before this did cause issue. I hemmed and hawed on how to bring this up with Ray, who was not only my boss, but the co-owner of BioWare without getting a ton of people in trouble, or worse yet, having to introduce some draconian "Don't play games during work hours" mandate which no one wanted. I slowly walked down the long hallway towards Ray's office not relishing the impending conversation, and I began to hear swearing coming from his open door. *Great,* I thought, *he's already pissed at something. This is going to be fun.* As I get closer to his office I start to hear more detail beyond the profanity (and Ray rarely swears). "Damn succubus, didn't even drop a decent item!" and "That was my last healing potion too!". As I entered into his office proper, I already knew what was up but seeing him in a multiplayer game of *Diablo* with my lead designer and others of the team confirmed two things. First, no one is going to be in any trouble and second, *Diablo* had conquered BioWare completely.

We did learn a lot from *Diablo*, however. We were using a lot of standard real-time strategy controls and interfaces for our game which few had done before, and *Diablo* proved we were on the right path by using similar designs in a number of areas . They also used "quick items"— items in your inventory that could instantly be used by hitting a hotkey. These limited number of slots would be filled with potions and scrolls, making the game infinitely more action orientated without having to fumble with an inventory screen in order to access these often used items. *Baldur's Gate* did not have this, but after playing *Diablo*, we realised not having this (now) obvious feature would be a huge mistake. Of course, there were also downsides to this *Diablo* exposure—*Baldur's Gate* was at least two weeks late shipping because of our crippling addiction (and I am being very, *very* conservative...).

Another feature that was amazingly not intended originally for the *Baldur's Gate* series was the "press spacebar to pause game". While paused you can give orders, go into inventories, etc., and plan the next moves for your party. Originally the game was going to be fully "real-time" where players controlled each character as a real-time strategy game such as *Age of Empires*. The ability to pause the game was a debug tool the programmers and designers put in to check out code and features, and never intended for anything else; however, after playing with it enabled for months and watching others play, we noticed that everyone used it. Every player would run characters around, see an enemy, pause the game, issue orders for up to six of their characters, select unpause, and let it play out. If things got hairy everyone paused the game, considered their options, and unpaused once figuring out their game plan. There were almost no exceptions—everyone played this way and had fun. We discussed what it would take to make this a supported feature and implement properly. We ended up adding pause as a full feature and expanding it by adding auto-pause conditions the player can configure. If you see a trap or an enemy, etc., the game can automatically pause so the player can figure out what they want to do first before acting. Even though you never have to pause and can play the game completely in real-time, I have never heard anyone playing this way. Thinking we originally intended real-time play as the only option boggles my mind. This has become a standard mechanic for not just many BioWare games but has filtered into many others as well across many genres and was just a happy accident.

Understand scheduling

Much like programming, you need to understand the limitations when creating any design. You may not be responsible for the schedule creation or maintenance, but are beholden to it. This is doubly true if you are in design— much of the team is "downstream" and need your work before starting their projects. The disciplines art, design, and programming are unpredictable on some level, partly because each is very creative. You are doing something that most likely no one has ever done before and at the very least in a way that accommodates the rest of the game, which is unique. Initial documentation is also only the first step in design. Implementation via the tools is another aspect, and perhaps the most time consuming is the balancing and tweaking after these first two steps are complete. Whether it's adjusting balance of weapons or other gameplay to fixing bugs, typos, or overhauling full sections to make them more fun, design is active from the first day to the very last moment before the game ships. Some of your time is also spent working closely with the programmers and artists, explaining what you need even after the first documentation is completed. I have found that spending a little bit of time up front when a concept is about to start or a feature is about to be implemented can save huge amounts of time. Assumptions are rife in most design documents which generally are the source of many later issues. Team members are not mind readers often working on that feature in a vacuum and don't know how it fits into the larger whole. As the designer, make sure it's clear what is needed through documentation, illustration, or discussion. It is quite literally your job.

Knowing it when you see it: What is Art?

A great example of a concept artist is one of the first I ever worked with—John Gallagher. He was a very early hire for BioWare, coming from a film and TV background. In fact I think John met owners Ray and Greg when he was sent over for a local news/entertainment show interview about the new company, and they basically talked about games and other interests they shared. Not before long, he was part of the team and playing a key role.

Every square inch of John's office was covered with concepts. Every wall had the latest and greatest completed. On the back wall was an entire hand drawn layout... A map showcasing the world of *Baldur's Gate*. It was maybe six or seven feet across and showed every alley, business, temple, and tavern. He had shelves with all sorts of reference books (the Internet was still early in its infancy) of weapons, armour, and building styles along with artist reference books, comics, and any other artsy or geeky reference you can imagine. The room was dominated by a tall drafting table that John was pretty much constantly standing or sitting behind. He had a computer but rarely used it for work— hundreds of coloured markers and pencils were his main tools.

John's drawings were quite detailed. As an artist, you could see his progression not just in style but adapting key details that the 3D modellers needed to continue building the world. The perspective was not always ideal or too much detail in some areas, but his artwork was both consistent and fast. I have rarely worked with a prodigious and proliferate artist as John. He could have an interior done in a few hours, ready for the next step. With a huge amount of content in the *Baldur's Gate* series, there would have been few that could have accomplished the amazing level of visualization.

He was also an entertaining and funny guy. A few years older than us, he had real world experience and was rude, crude, and more than willing to talk about any topic or escapade. This was endlessly fascinating to us, and it was great working with him in general. I would end up in his office to see how the latest concepts were going, and we would end up talking and laughing about the latest weekend adventures, or some story about movie theories or super hero concepts. A 15 minute "check in" would turn into an hour while John sketched with pencils or one of the seemingly endless coloured markers across paper. He was never losing time over these chats, but I was. It was worth it.

John's workflow was basically getting a rough text description from a game designer. Outlined was the bare minimum for an interior with any quest items or points of interest required for whatever happened in the area during the game. Sometimes it was well detailed with lots of requirements by the designer. Other times the text would be "Medium sized, single floor inn interior, cozy, fireplace, and room for a few dozen to sit", leaving John to make the visualization work logically and fit in style-wise with the location. Each town had a theme or building style with Elves building differently from Drow (Dark Elves) and Dwarves. From a poor farming village or ancient 800 year old library, he drew it all. John drew every single location in Baldur's gate, every square inch. I wonder where all those concepts are now?

As projects get larger, the one area that seems to continue growing the most is art. The sheer scope and scale of the raw assets that go into the game is staggering. Each new generation of gaming consoles offers more processing power, allowing for more polygons on the screen at a time and increasing the amount of texture memory by many, many multiples compared to a few years ago. This means more detailed and complex art is being created which adds more people and time to create. Each project and team has different requirements for art, but I will break down broad areas of that remain fairly constant in game creation.

Art Director

The Art Director is in charge of the direction and productivity of the entire art team, making sure the art is consistent in both quality and conformity for what the game needs. They also set that direction initially and work very closely with the Design Director, Programming Director, and Creative Director in all aspects of the game. Responsible for scheduling the team's time, they may also create content for the game depending on the team size.

Concept artist

This is an artist that works often in 2D with pencil and paper, although in recent years I am seeing more working with Wacom tablets and their software of choice (Adobe Photoshop, Adobe Illustrator etc). They design the look and feel of the concept which is then passed along to another artist for creating the game assets. Working closely with the Art Director and Creative Director, concept artists are at the top of the art pipeline. Everything from specific characters, weapons to mood paintings for level concepts start with a concept. Key traits for this position are having a good eye for getting essential elements conveyed, working well with others, taking direction, and generally creating concepts fast.

Character modeller

As the title implies, this artist tends to specialize on character creation. This is usually a more technical focus as animation rigs and other aspects have to be kept in mind when modelling a character. Knowing and understanding the context in which a model is used influences a great deal on how things are created. The process is quite different depending if the model's face is used as a close-up during an in-game cutscene versus a background character in a crowd scene. You need to have the ability to work from concepts and multiple detail levels as well as understand the fundamentals of proportion, anatomy etc.

Character modelling work is front and centre in the game, and often the huge parts of the game revolve around staring at these models, so the quality really matters. Some games the "character" may not be human or even humanoid but a vehicle, other protagonist, antagonist, or general challenge to the player. Some modellers specialise, but it is wise to have a broad spectrum of subject matter as possible since not all games or companies exactly focus on your specialty. Important for this role is technical skill, and the ability to understand complex concepts like proportions and tool knowledge.

Animator

This can refer to a person that creates ingame or cutscene animations. Animators are in separate teams and treated more as a central resource for a whole studio rather than being attached to a specific title, but as the scope of animation has continued growing, more are permanently added to the game art team. Having a traditional background (2D) is a huge plus,, and the best animators not only know the tools but honed the same fundamentals as any animator of traditional Disney films .

This has become further specialised because of larger teams and features like weapons animation have become a "thing". Also, keep in mind that games have all sorts of types of viewpoints. You may end up doing first person animations (the player is the protagonist and sees the game from his/her point of view), or third person (the player is watching the character interact), or any combination depending on the genre of game.

The position of animator does not always mean 3D. Many games require animated 2D elements. Depending on the platform, the entire game's assets and gameplay may be animated in 2D. An animator position can mean many things, but each revolves around motion and moving elements in order to improve gameplay and believability of the game world.

Level Artist

This position dances on the line between game design and art on many projects. In some game studios, the Level Designers create the gameplay block outs and pass along the specifications to Level Artists who take the gameplay stub[1] and concept art to create an environment that looks amazing and engaging while maintaining the gameplay. In other studios, both the layout and art for a level is created by one person. It depends a great deal on the needs of the game and skillset of the artist.

Level Artists can create content on other platforms such as 2D games, puzzle games (think *Angry Birds* for mobile), and anything in-between. When creating levels in situations such as these Level Artists are every bit designers as artists.

---

[1] A gameplay stub is just the very basics of the gameplay intended. It is unpolished and meant to be a way to test an idea without committing too many resources.

2D or User Interface (UI) Artist

Artists with graphic design backgrounds do well in this area. In every game, there is a barrier between the player and the game— the user interface. The slicker, easier, and more intuitive the UI can be, the more the player can be immersed in the game. This is a huge challenge that most games fail in some aspect. Whether it's indecipherable icons, clunky menu-flows, or unclear messaging of game events, it is very easy to take a misstep and ruin the game experience for players. To be fair, coming up with 200 legible, unmistakeable icons showing sci-fi concepts and powers is far from simple. Games with deep mechanics need to convey an awful lot of information to the player in order to survive, let alone have fun. Developing an informative and clear UI is a huge challenge. UI Artists are worth their weight in gold, and the industry seems to be short on skilled people.

UI artists also are heavily into design and responsible for tone, flow, and readability for every menu in the game. Menus are not just what the player sees when starting up the game. Depending on the game, menus are everywhere and part of core gameplay: when a player upgrades, progresses, wins, and loses; objectives change or update; Their scores or standing locally and globally; and players interact with friends and the world. Every single screen in a game had some significant problems to solve by an UI Artist. Great artists solve these problems so well that players do not even notice their work. Games can sink or swim on how well an UI Artist does their job. The first 15 minutes can be instantly destroyed because a player gets lost in what is going on and is largely the responsibility of the UI Artists and Designers to make sure this never happens.

Other aspects about making art in games

Making art to schedule: This is a concept I try to get across whenever I do talks at universities and schools— art needs to get done on time. There are plenty of very skilled artists who just can't work to a schedule and do not have a place in the games industry. Time management is something that needs to be learned, and just because you do not feel "creative" does not matter in the least. An artist is assigned "X" art to be done in "Y" period of time, and a game will never be completed if they do not have the ability to accomplish this requirement.

Know your tools: Much like programmers, artists cannot get across saying/showing a concept without mastering the medium they need to work in. The tools change developer to developer, so in the end having skills in most of the basic software packages will always be useful.

Know your limits and budgets: When creating an asset a modeller should have a budget for polygons, triangles, texture memory, or other relevant measuring metrics for the asset. If the Art Director did not provide a metric then the modeller should get it from the Graphics or Lead Programmer, and if they don't have a budget to work within expect trouble. Nothing is worse than creating an epic and masterful character and then being told "Can you remove two-thirds of the polygons, thanks". So much pain and suffering from optimization at the end of a project can be avoided by determining and adhering to a metric budget.

My favourite story about the follies in ignoring or not understanding the context of creating content revolves around a game called *Daikatana* that was released in 2000. In this rather infamous story, an artist worked for months on the texture for an arrowhead. The end result was an arrow texture 1300 x 960 pixels on an object that would never be more than a few pixels on the screen. The final texture probably took about ten minutes to make at 1/100th of the resolution and complexity, looking no different to the overkill version in the game.

A piece of art, from start to finish

For this example we will use a character model as an example in an AAA PC game. Every platform is different, and team structures vary greatly depending on size, skills, and budgets. This is one an example to give you a good idea for an average flow from idea to game asset.

1) Design: There will be a game design that calls for a certain character. It will be a contained design document, usually in text format with a description and attributes in game terms, and include reference art, Google search images, etc., made by the designer. It will then be approved and/or moved by the Lead Designer or Creative Director to the Art Director and Concept Artist.

2) Concept: The design document detailing the character is taken by the Concept Artist and drawn usually in 2D or painted using their preferred software package. Concepts are also commonly still drawn on paper at this stage—it really is up to the artist. The Concept Artist takes this idea that is little more than a collection of text and reference images, and collates into a visualization that makes sense for the game by matching style and proportion while adding their unique flair. There is often much latitude, but in general the Concept Artist works with the Designer to ensure the aspects that matter to the design are taken into account and included. The Art Director or

Creative Director signs off on the final piece, making sure consistency and other requirements are met.

3) Model The finalized concept is passed along to another artist, the 3D modeller. The software used varies a great deal and is constantly evolving, but within the 3D package the modeller takes the concept and creates the raw in-game asset. In general they must follow the concept faithfully, but there are times when back-and-forth for both artistic and technical reasons happen, and the model character must be changed. The Designer should be involved with these discussions in case there are impacts on the rest of the game design. Changing a weapon, stance, or other elements means the asset no longer fits its intended purpose. Don't forget that in parallel the Designer is working with programmers, and other artists etc., on the features for the character in the game. Communication and referencing the concept art is important to creating a model that fits in the game. The Art Director often signs off on the model, checking that the technical requirements are met. At this point, the model is untextured and flat, needing a "skin".

4) Texturing: The next step is texturing the model. This is sometimes done by the modellers that have the skillset, but most often a separate artist will take the signed-off model and add texture. Software packages vary but the end result is a textured model of a

character that looks exactly the same as the concept image from step two except now as a game ready asset. Again the Art Director usually signs off to ensure all requirements are met.

5) Animation: Animation is broken down into several steps or areas to be completed by one person or a team. First the model must be "boned"— a skeleton is added showing where and how the model is allowed to move before the actual animations can be created. Some games have another step that utilises motion capture, or "mo-cap", where actors perform the movements in the real world, their positions tracked and recorded by software to be used as the base for the in-game animations. Even with this step, animators must take the information and "clean it up" which is very work intensive but often gives more realistic results. This practice is especially good for consistency in a story driven game where an actor can truly perform not just the voice but the motions and emotions of his/her character. This is again signed off by the Art Director once completed.

6) Into the game: The character asset is checked in, and hopefully the code support and design is ready at the same time. Now the character can be used in game for the first time.

Considering each step can take weeks for a single asset, you can see why some development teams are so large, and why it takes years to finish a game. This is just one model not including effects, weapons, abilities, code support, audio, or the countless other features that make an asset considered "game final".

Marketing: Where toys and crazy ideas reside

Soldier of Fortune II: Double Helix is a video game licensed from the magazine of the same name about being a soldier for hire, fighting in all sorts of high-risk scenarios. Serious gun research helped make the gameplay authentic, and players could utilise a wide range of modern weaponry for all sorts of ultraviolence—this game still stands out as the most violent I have ever worked on. The team even went out in the Arizona desert with real soldiers of fortune and shot all sorts of weapons ranging from the standard to the ridiculous. But how do you promote such a game touting features with those aspects? Activision marketing thought it would be a good idea having the *Soldier of Fortune II* logo and text of the game put on the side of a .50 caliber round and mailed along with press event invites to journalists. For those of you not versed with the actual size of a .50 caliber, it is a monster at 20 mm in diameter and 138 mm long (.804 x 5.45 inches long).

Well, let me tell you the American postal service is not huge fans of sending nationally and especially internationally using their service, decommissioned rounds or not. We also gave away a ton of these bullets at the E3 tradeshow later that same year to fans and press over the five days we were showing off the game. I bet a lot of attendees had "some explaining to do" at the airports as their bags were scanned, revealing the largest and most powerful ammunition available in the world tucked in next to the toothpaste. Heck I had a handful on me still in my laptop bag when going to my next airport trip and nearly forgot about them. Glad I dumped them and avoid seeming like I was trying to invade the host nation rather than taking a simple business trip.

If you walk down the hallway in a major publisher and enter into an office, you see posters, trinkets, awards, and boxes of games both new and old. Most likely every cool toy related to games, items sent out to the press, and special editions of various games are strewn across every flat surface in the room. You have just entered the marketing person's domain. The range of items marketing stamps a game's name on is truly staggering: statues and figurines, sports equipment, clothing, to the more exotic like swords. Name any physical object and at some point a marketing person thought it was a good idea to brand with their product somehow... and that other people would like to have a branded version as a keepsake.

Many people have no idea what marketing a game really means which includes most people in the games industry. Some think marketing is about coming up with great ideas on how to sell a game or developing ads that grab attention which is partly right, but the vast majority of the tough work that Marketing does is crunch numbers: looking at profit and loss benchmarks for various competing games and analysing different magazines, ads, and other media that a company can market a game. Marketing serves as the key point of contact for many of the different issues for distributing and selling the game around the world, meaning analysis of more statistics but from different countries and territories, each with their own twist and requirements.

I have had such an amazing range of experiences with marketing that it is hard to define what is considered the norm. It boils down to the marketing person you get and honestly your responsibility as a game developer to ensure that relationship is strong and productive.

Every publisher has different criteria hiring for Marketing, but for me the number one thing required is that the person cares and understands gaming. "WHAT?!A person whose job it is to promote and get people excited about a game may not like games?". It happens far more often than you would imagine. Apparently some publishers look at marketing as a broad skill and product independent. If you have created a campaign for razor blades, you can create one for diapers or the next first-person shooter. I cannot describe how much I utterly disagree with this concept. The Marketing person does not have to be a hardcore gamer to "get it" or do the job well, but understanding the product they are trying to market helps significantly. Diapers or some sort of confection is much easier to understand more quickly and intuitively than a video game, which is trying to be new or different in some way from those before them. Diving into message boards regarding a favourite game, you will see that the target audience has very specific tastes and are fickle about nearly every aspect of the games they play. One false word or slant even perceived regarding the game and can have an insurrection of people shouting on the internet louder than any marketing campaign.

Some of my worst experiences were with marketing folks who did not or care to understand the product and did not push to ensure the campaign was successful—people who only get behind "easy winners" and do nothing to add support. I am amazed to think that people still don't understand that we as a team are responsible for making winners. No one else is just going to fix and make it better, and our impact on whatever we touch should be to strive and push beyond what anyone else thinks is possible. This is not exclusive to marketing, but I have witnessed more of this apathy here than most other areas. I think mainly this is due to a lack of comprehension, making it hard to get behind the project. Better to depend on easy to understand projects and general sentiment than put your neck on the line. I can see how someone can take this ambivalent approach, but it is the worst decision for the quality and success of a project.

How to have the best relationship with Marketing in three easy steps

1) Support: Be ready for last minute asset and event requests. Every team complains that Marketing is always asking for things last minute. Even with a great plan worked out with asset delivery lists created for the whole campaign, Marketing (if doing their job right) will find these last minute opportunities that can really help a project: some magazine cancels a cover story and needs a new one, a press event has an unexpected slot open, or Microsoft started a promotion and wants to do some cross-marketing. These are good, even great, but rolling with the request is often hard since game projects do not have any spare time, let alone last minute marketing. Best to plan budgeting time of a person (or people) on the team to support Marketing. Have an outsourcing company ready for the real binds—there are many great ones that in a pinch can save your ass.

A great example and credit to the developer was in *Crysis 2* when Marketing wanted a series of movies showing multiplayer gameplay. These were not small productions: hours and hours of raw footage needed to be recorded, editing, music tracks licensed, logos, etc. Each requirement needed to be done well before the game was complete. Our initial recordings were at EA in Guildford, UK, but the code was not ready and takes finesse from the team to look its best when the game is incomplete. The best bet was recording at Crytek Nottingham which could be a huge disruption for everyone. Marketing hired an editor, and travelled with him to help with the set-up. We commandeered a goodly section of the onsite QA and cinematic employees from Crytek for days at a time to storyboard, shoot, edit, and mix the videos.

By the second video, everyone had gotten into the groove and became fairly efficient. This only happened because Marketing stepped up and searched for other solutions, and the developer made major concessions and worked exceedingly close with Marketing. Everyone ended ahead as the videos where a major factor in the campaign with millions of views that helped spread the word and get the masses excited.

2) Keep them Informed and involved: The best practice is to ensure Marketing is informed constantly, regardless of their background or previous product experience by meeting regularly and starting early in the project. Show builds and have play tests. Don't treat Marketing like a necessary evil, or they will become alienated and everyone suffers the consequences. Engage Marketing by walking through the key points of the game, explaining what is special and unique. Don't forget to provide examples and show code. This meeting is face–to-face to increase their understanding of the game, not some bulleted email sent a year out from shipping. By failing to convince the Marketing team why your game is amazing and needs to be marketed, there is no way anyone in the real world is going to get excited. Marketing will also have insight into other industry projects and can help tailor the message a great deal.

3) Keep them on side: Nothing is gained by leaving out the Marketing team or worse yet, they view the project consistently negatively. They are the spokespeople for the game to everyone within the publisher, press, and other industry connections over drinks, which can push or sink momentum. Once on board and excited, Marketing will reach and push, accomplishing far more. A great marketing campaign does not guarantee success, but success is almost impossible without one.

My impressions of Marketing when I first started making games was not that positive—I saw them more of a hindrance, like a sword of Damocles, threatening to unleash some horrible feature request in order to "sell more units". Back in the earlier days, these requests did happen from time to time. I remember on the first game I worked on, *Shattered Steel*, we were going over what the box should resemble. Endless rounds of art went back-and-forth with different logos and robots (the game was about a mechanized warfare and giant robots), and it was all starting to blur. Marketing emailed the development team wanting the box cover to have a more "human" feel because empathizing with a robot is hard, followed by a fax they felt should "do the trick". About five minutes later a fax come through (this was 1996). As it printed, top to bottom: *Yup, there is the logo we all seemed to agree on... There is the top of the robot and... What... What is that?!* Painted crudely were eyes and lips on the robot. I am not talking about the WWII fighter plane with jagged shark teeth, eyes, and lips painted on the nose tip. Big, pouty lips and fake eyelashes covered the robot as if in drag, not that I know what gender these robots should be or anything. As each line was printed and more of the image scrolled down, the more confused, angry, and well more confused we felt. To this day, I still do not know if it was a joke or real. After working with Marketing folks for the last 18 games, I would like to think it was a very tired person who saw just one too many drafts of that box cover …

Since then I have been lucky enough to work with many talented and patient Marketing folks, and learned a great deal about the industry from them. It takes a certain type of knowledge to understand both the medium of the product and the type of medium to promote the game. More now than ever the market is a global one, and the understanding of each unique market is a challenge that a developer could not ever grasp on their own.

QA: Gatekeepers and gamers

The messiest, most painful release I have ever been a part of was *Call of Duty: Finest Hour*. The sheer number of people involved, multiple teams, and terrible initial decisions that came back to haunt us on mainly every front... it became my benchmark for "pain" and has ever since. In fact, I invoke its memory whenever I am shipping a game that seems like a mess. I literally ask myself "Is this as bad as *Call of Duty: Finest Hour*? Nope? Ok cool, we can do this". This game was the first console version of *Call of Duty* many lessons to learn: new and different code bases for both single player and multiplayer that required the game to shut down and restart when switching between modes, terrible performance, and bugs, bugs, bugs. I want to claim most of the issues were in the single player but that would be lying—we had nearly as many "showstoppers" in multiplayer, the part I was responsible for.

As the team approached Beta version, the game was in a sad state, but we sent it to the first parties[1] for precertification as a heads-up that this was coming in late, fast, and needed to be approved quickly. Keep in mind the team had an excellent relationship with these parties, and we all benefited when a good game ships. When a game's development is in trouble, we all suffer, and our team was basically asking for help us. They looked and played the game in its current state, and responded with "We can't help if you can't even help yourselves". Yes, the game was in that bad of shape. It was "all hands on deck", and a Herculean effort was made by literally everyone involved to get it shipped on time with as few bugs as possible. Anyone who had a heartbeat at Activision was roped into working on this game. Meeting the deadline involved major sacrifice: employees did not go home for weeks on end or sleep, and did nothing that resembled self-preservation. Industry veterans who had made and shipped dozens of games before talked openly about quitting after the release. Yes, it was that painful.

QA was aware from the very beginning and told us, helping everywhere they could but "reality" could not be ignored. They advised months we would never hit Alpha version on time and weeks before Beta version we were nowhere near the required

---

[1] Sony and Microsoft.

quality. The team had a good understanding from their insight but refused to believe it. QA knows—they always know. Like Santa Claus with gamertags[2], you can't pull one over on QA.

Quality assurance or QA, is one of the most underappreciated aspects of game development. Beyond the long hours, repetitive tasks, and being forced to play genuinely unfun games (as games are before they are done), the job is thankless. Treated as an entry level position in the industry, the role does attract all kinds of people. From the wannabe designers to students looking for summer work, the range of personalities within QA are the broadest found in any department. Many senior development staff, especially production, started in QA, and even with these roots, QA is still much maligned.

I personally think it is because QA resemble the police. Police in general are great folk no matter where, but they show up on the worst day of your life. Rarely does someone talk to a cop when everything is going well—usually it's when something bad happened or is about to occur. Most people can't help but start associating negative things with the police solely from doing their job. QA is like that—rarely having good news, complaining and pointing out

---

[2] Gamertags are handles or names that players use to identify themselves online.

the bad parts of the game a team has passionately slaved over for months and years. Regardless of the naysaying, QA is one of the most important partners in not only shipping the game but releasing a great game. Short of the designers making the game, no one will have more intimate knowledge in the inner workings of the game and this should remembered far more often.

Understanding what QA can do for the project and how best to use their time is important. Within a publisher, QA is a shared resource between multiple projects—wasting their time can be expensive and hurt more than just your game. I found that the leads of QA worry as much if not more about budgets and dependencies than any other group. Partly due to the lack of focus QA usually receives from upper management, the department has to fight and scrape for any support and resources. The other part is that the people I have been fortunate enough to work with in QA are exceedingly passionate.

What does QA do?

QA's involvement starts early but does not come into full effect until Alpha. Once concept for the game is created, QA can rough out a draft budget, and get a better grasp on scope and prepare for when they join the project: developing testing plans and systems test outlines, and preparing any additional testing that may be required due to specific features of the project. QA becomes quiet and inactive while development sorts out the prototype and starts the main production phase.

Onsite[3] QA can start well before Alpha. A small QA team can be very effective when working in close proximity with development. When both teams are onsite, QA can ensure the build properly functions for playtests, work directly with development team members for testing specific features that are being implemented, and in general help keep the builds healthy and provide additional development support.

Alpha is when QA gets into full swing. Alpha is defined when features for the game are complete—each major playable component of the game is achieved. Art may change, and optimisations in performance and other aspects to make the game "better" may happen, but fundamentally the game is playable. QA can start providing proper bug lists, feature reviews, and feedback on how fun the game is, which serves as the major checkpoint and sign off whether the game lifecycle has reached Alpha. In most companies,

---

[3] Onsite: Located with the developer of the game.

QA indicates whether Alpha stage is achieved and signs off, not the Producer, Creative Director, or anyone else. In fact, this team certifies all phases of the game's development from this point and onwards. From Alpha, QA will run through their checklists on each build, usually taking upwards of a week to complete a pass on a build depending on the size and complexity of the game. The bug database is set up beforehand and shared with the developer, and now used in earnest.

The next big milestone for QA is Beta stage. Beta is defined as each asset in the game is available and locked: art, audio, and every other requirement as defined by Alpha is present and functional. At this stage, the dev teams are only allowed to fix bugs and optimise for performance. Once again QA certifies whether the build qualifies to achieve Beta, and if yes, now game development enters the final push to ship a game. During this time, first parties (e.g. Nintendo, Microsoft, Sony) will get access to the game shipping on their consoles, which is called precertification. These companies have their own QA with a set of guidelines that each game must pass in order to sell and play on the hardware.

To ship a game, QA has to sign off that every bug is closed at this point which is not straightforward. I am confident in saying games are so incredibly complex that none ever has shipped with zero bugs. Development has a threshold of allowable issues that are categorises bugs in different ways depending on the company, but in general involve similar requirements: zero "A" class bugs (crashes and game stoppers), zero "B" class bugs (graphical errors, broken gameplay that is very noticeable but not a game stopper), and few "C" bugs as possible (considered minor—everything else basically). QA will not sign off shipping a game if even one "A" class bug exists, but depending on schedules and other pressures, "B" bugs can be negotiated if addressed in a future patch or update. "C" bugs always exist in a shipped game, the amount depending on how much time the dev team has set aside in the end phases to fix issues. In an ideal world, Alpha is three months, Beta one month, and then the game is released. This almost never happens. I have seen game development running very late go from Alpha to Beta to release in just a few weeks. This shortened timeframe is a gamble not worth taking most times, and there are whole YouTube channels dedicated to people playing very broken games in humorous ways.

Once the publisher QA has signed off, the game goes off for a final submission to the first parties. When precertification is complete with feedback. fixing items highlighted by the first party is usually straight forward; however,. this is not always the case, and sometimes issues must be fixed and resubmitted. Each cycle costs time and money, which is scary when facing hard deadlines. First parties are our partners, but they have a quality bar they must be maintained for obvious reasons.

Audio: The other half of your gaming experience

Choosing music for a game is never easy. Not only are there normal budgetary concerns, finding a good composer that understands not only the thematic needs but technical limitations and other requirements is challenging. Making music for a game is very different than composing for a movie or TV show. In *Baldur's Gate*, we needed the music written in "chunks", where a piece could transition into or out of another section. The team wanted to have a nice background theme as the player walked through a forest transition into a battle theme when reaching a fight scenario and back to the previous theme once the attack concluded. Since a section of music could translate into nearly any other section, this task was insanely difficult and time consuming to put together. Honestly the audio and music folks in most games do not get enough credit, their work making or breaking the tone of every single scene.

    Black Isle Studios (Interplay) who published *Baldur's Gate* did a fantastic job of organising and providing music to us but not in a timely manner. The dev team was far along in development and still had no music. The folks at Interplay had sample tracks but for whatever reason, were sitting on the music and not passing along. I had heard (and approved) some brief clips and knew they were good, but had no idea why it was taking so long. So after a few weeks of back and forth, we decided to force their hand. The dev told them that in order to test our sound code, memory usage, etc., we needed the music or would put in our own... and we promised it would not be good music. This was a believable enough excuse to force Activision's hand, but they laughed and said basically "go ahead" jokingly, adding "how bad could it be?".

Challenge accepted. We looked around, discussed, and decided. The next build QA received had only one track that played "The Smurfs" theme song in all instances requiring music (which was constantly) at unreasonably loud volume with the audio controls "accidentally" broken and removed. Within minutes of the build being installed at Interplay, I imagined a panicked and not amused QA lead rushing upstairs into Chris Parker's office (our Producer) screaming bloody murder. I am not 100% sure what the real reaction internally was, but Interplay sent the audio over very quickly afterwards if I recall correctly. We reciprocated by sending a new build.

Audio is an offshoot of design and every bit important as any system design. Nothing contributes more to the "feel" of any situation, whether a piece of action is playing out or a story beat is being portrayed, than the audio and music. In the past, audio engineers (I consider them designers) were brought on laughably late to a project, usually during post Alpha (which is after all the features are done), which means doing what they can in a system and world already created. Over the years this has improved but is still one of the most overlooked aspects of designing a good product. From button "clicks" to dialogue, there is never a time this feature is not in front of the player and should be treated with the same weight as graphics, system design, and any other core element.

So what do these audio people actually do? Well if brought in at a relevant time, this role can help shape the audio features which is how music and sound tell the narrative. If audio doesn't receive get the tools they need or implemented in an efficient way, the game suffers. This process is made easier if the tech/engine has a decent backbone for audio. The audio team wants to have the right "hooks" in the game from design or code to do what they want. This varies a great deal depending on the project, but I found meeting regularly with the sound engineers, and spending the time and overhead greatly multiplied the quality of the game.

Voice over recording

Then there is the voice over (VO) recording. I have had the pleasure to sit in quite a few recording sessions for various games and watch the skill of a good Voice Over Director—it's incredible. They hear things mortals just can't. A "popped P" or the slightest background noise that I would have missed they catch. Speed, cadence, matching accents and voices from lines recorded days or even months earlier, they catch it. Voice Over Directors are musicians of the highest order, getting the performance from voice actors at the level required with seemingly effortless, pure direction. Knowing when to push an actor, try a different approach, or tweak an element to make it sound better during the session, their skillset is amazing. With the proper information and context of what needs to be recorded in regards to the game, when the audio is integrated back into the game, the end result is quite magical and overall game experience is improved.

The Voice Over Actors are also amazing and worth mentioning. There are only a few hundred "regular" SAG (the Screen Actors Guild) Voice Over Actors in the Los Angeles area where most game VO is recorded in AAA games. I am constantly astonished by what these people can do. They almost universally look normal and unassuming, but in front of a microphone they perform magic. I mean it. These actors don't have one voice but dozens, each with their own use that be modified to suit a role. When providing voice direction, I would give examples of actors or flavours, some of them nearly nonsensical like a Texan Sean Connery to get the tone, and they do it. I will get back a confident and brash Sean Connery in a perfect Irish accent of your choice. Yes, there are many different Irish accents, and the actor and director can do the one needed. "No, more south rural please", and they will do the line again. It's a magnificent thing to behold watching a proper professional perform anything to that level of expertise. Also, we work with Hollywood stars as it has become fairly commonplace for big actors to voice video games. Sitting in a sound booth hearing acting legends say things like "Arrrrgh. Mah spleeeen!!!" can be hilarious. I may or may not have written silly lines just to get famous people to say ridiculous things.

Games have hundreds of characters, and nearly all AAA games have every line recorded with voice over, which is a lot of content to record, edit, and master. The end result transforms the game, making it believable and helping with suspension of disbelief. Players know what a bad line of VO can do to their gaming experience, instantly recognising whether a game is amateur or professional. It's worth spending the time and money to get a good performance.

Sound effects

A great example of the impact sounds make was during an internal play test of the first-person shooter *Crysis 2*. We kept getting feedback from QA and others that the shotgun was weak. We poured over data showing kill rates, loadout[1] values, and other information that help us make the game balanced. The data showed the shotgun was located was in a good place, and damage was a bit high but within the norms of other games. We played a few matches, specifically paying close attention to the shotgun. The weapon designer was spot-on, stating it was performing correctly but sounded a bit "weedy" instead of the powerful, loud sound expected. I talked to the weapons designer and said, "Hey, work with the audio guy and just turn up the bass on the audio when you fire. Give it some oomph". After the adjustment in audio, we did not divulge details beyond "we fixed it". Only the weapons designer, audio

---

[1] Loadouts is a game term where a player chooses what equipment to bring out into the gaming world. Usually the amount of equipment is limited so this choice is important in deciding how they will play.

engineer, and I knew what was done. The next day during another play test with nothing changed and the same gameplay values, QA was saying "Holy crap, you may have boosted the damage too much! In our next studio wide playtest the shotgun was by far the most chosen and used in the loadouts, and people where having a blast!". Pardon the pun—audio matters.

The user interface audio is 50% of the feedback while playing a game and isn't noticed most of the time . In almost every first-person shooter, there is a "sound" when a weapon hits which is subtle and unrealistic but provides feedback. Also, there is a separate sound, usually slightly higher pitch, to indicate a critical hit (headshot or similar depending on the game) and notify the shot was on point. I have sat with designers for hours deciding the sound, volume, and pitch, trying to make these elements fit within the game universe but just noticeable to pick up while not standing out or being annoying. Now imagine this for every single action in the game: footsteps, reloads, passive voice overs providing hints to what the other players or NPCs around are doing, confirmation button clicks in UI, and announcements of awards, progress, or impressive gameplay feats accomplished. Each has carefully crafted and considered audio that plays a key role in evoking a certain feel and emotion.

This audio helps set the tone and mood for every moment of the game. Much like scoring a movie or TV show, the music and sound effects chosen can make or kill the desired mood in any particular part of the game. A great music crescendo at the right moment in a plot point or an extra creepy creaking door sound to raise tension are in the control of a good audio designer. Try playing a favourite game with the sound off— so much flavour and communication on what is happening will be lost, and you start developing a sense on how much impact these men and women have in creating the actual feel of the game.

Music

We have come a long way from the "bleeps and bloops" of early game music. Brilliant composers, pulled from all aspects of the entertainment industry, use full orchestras and huge budgets to create some of the best musical scores in any medium. Big blockbuster movies and games spend the same amount of time and effort in their creation, usually employing the same talented musicians. Music is most likely the single largest tone-setter in any game. From the first loading screen to the crescendo of a plot point, how and where music is used tells the player how to feel in a subtle but focused way. Game soundtracks are released alongside games as downloadable on iTunes and other distributors, and win awards and recognised for their importance and contribution.

Games such as the *Grand Theft Auto* series license music from artists for specific genres to set very precise tones to great effect. The feel for *Grand Theft Auto: Vice City* came 90% from the amazing 1980s soundtrack selected. I probably played twice as long than usual because "that song" came on my character's car stereo, and I had to just keep cruising around until it was over. Using music from artists does not come cheap with games allocating huge parts of their budgets to license these tracks. This route has become standard for larger scale games.

Publisher and Developer relationships: Friendships and fistfights

What's in a name?

Naming a game is a frustrating process. Everyone gets involved, usually with too much passion. Naming your child is no less a feat, and naming a game feels on par with that level of commitment and importance. Of course that's crap. If I have learned one thing, the name on a personal preference level is mind numbingly unimportant. The marketing point of view differs, but whether someone likes the name or not, it really doesn't matter.

Baldur's Gate is a great example. The working title for the game was FRGX, as in *Forgotten Realms* Game "X". On all the design docs, database headers, code, etc., this was the moniker. The dev team was getting closer to discussing the game with the outside world but still did not have an official name. Now remember, BioWare was making the game, Interplay was publishing it, and TSR (soon to be Wizards of the Coast) owned the intellectual property, the *AD&D* universe, where the game was based. That's a lot of opinions and hoops to jump through to get a name approved, so taking time made sense. Naming went back-and–forth multiple times, basically with no conclusions... just 20 or so opinions. The process languished for weeks and months. Again we found ourselves closer to discussing the game with the outside world and still not having any proper reference for the game.

To force people's hands into making a decision, the dev team figured the best way was to change the working title to something so bad, so offensive that we would receive a finalized name. *But what is offensive and bad to everyone?* Within 10 minutes we had it. Dev started to rename documents, the splash screen for the game, etc., and sent a notification to Interplay via e-mail that the working title was changing from "FRGX" to "Christ Fucker" until we received a final name.

The reply was nearly instant, and the decision followed on very quickly: *Baldur's Gate*.

Now that we had a name, the irony was most of us hated *Baldur's Gate*. The name meant nothing to anyone unless you knew the lore and sounded boring. *It's a bloody town? A gate? It's a huge story about an evil God trying to destroy the world and uses the name of a city no one has heard of as the title?* But as we used

Baldur's Gate, talked about it, posted about it online, referenced it during interviews, and talked among ourselves using it... The name ceased to be a second rate town or empty title—it just was. Similar was when naming *Call of Duty*, and within Activision we were walking down the halls and saying "Hehehe, Doody". There was no way that name was going to stick as the final title, but of course it did and aside from the odd similar joke, no one thinks twice now. I worked on a real-time strategy (RTS) game called *Empires: Dawn of the Modern World,* and you should have seen the list of possible names. Rick Goodman was one of the brothers that made the original *Age of Empires* and now making this game independently in a new company for Activision. RTS names included the same three or four words, then a qualifying few that set the tone: *Age, Craft, Conquer, Rise*, and *Empire*. Mix and match as you please, and break out the thesaurus. In the end, the game scored a mid 80% of reviews with low sales. I am it was not the name's fault.

I have since learned this is the usual game naming process. A game becomes its own entity while the name is irrelevant to the game maker in the long term. It's just a noun, nothing more. Well, almost true. If the final name of *Baldur's Gate* stuck as *Christ Fucker*, I could concede that the name may have some impact on the game's perception.

I want to clarify that Interplay and BioWare had a great relationship during the creation of *Baldur's Gate.* From my end as both a Designer then Producer on the franchise, Interplay did nothing but support us, wanting the exact same goal as us—a great game. We got along personally as well; people like Fergus Urquhart, Chris Parker, and Doug Avery were colleagues and friends. I say this since sometimes what went back-and-forth may sound spiteful or actions done to people you hate, but much like best friends or brothers, it was for the entirely opposite reasons.

Every developer and publisher partnership is different, depending on the skillset. personalities of the people involved, and the requirements of the project. The deal terms between publishers and developers vary so greatly there is no "one" relationship, every instance is unique. Here are a few more examples

Relic Entertainment and Sierra

The relationship between a developer and publisher can be strained even when it has little to do with the project. In early 2000, I was at Relic Entertainment in Vancouver working on the *Homeworld* franchise. It was at this point the game publisher Sierra was going through serious turmoil as a company. Sierra was a venerated and well-established publisher from the early days.

Founded in 1979, the company survived many ups and downs in the industry over the years but was really struggling during this time. In the beginning of 1999, Sierra announced a major restructuring that meant layoffs and the closure of many internal studios. They managed to ship *Homeworld* during this upheaval, and the game won many critical awards and sold well.

In 2000 the changes continued with the acquisition of Sierra by Vivendi, a French mega conglomerate. At the time it seemed Vivendi would secure Sierra and its games, massive layoffs happened as well. The dev team was working diligently on *Homeworld 2* when this upheaval was happening, and one of the side effects was us getting paid for delivering milestones. This was not Sierra (now Vivendi) being difficult or lacked cash, and it wasn't Relic not fulfilling milestones or deliverables, it was that the staff on the Vivendi side was changing constantly. We would have a different Executive Producer or Marketing Manager every other week depending on who quit, was laid off, or fired. This made doing anything difficult. Relationships are 90% of this process, and having to again explain, show, and submit each deliverable every time someone changed positions at Vivendi started to become a full-time job. Dev once asked for an organisational chart of Vivendi so we could understand who was where now (every other time we got an email it seemed new names were on the CC list) and were told flat out "no". It was not a "no" because they did not wish to share the info but because they did not know the answers with the constant shifting. This continued for some time. We ended up putting *Homeworld 2* on a slow burn while working on prototypes of the game for consoles and other projects as the chaos was throwing everything into the air and nothing was guaranteed.

Activision and id Software

From all that I have written so far, you would assume the Publisher has the power from essentially holding the purse strings. This is true for the most part, but there are exceptions like id Software. The id Software/Activision relationship was long and profitable for both, and born from id Software making amazing tech and becoming famous within the industry to both publishers and fans alike as creating cutting edge and cool "things". Having their games within a stable of titles was a feather in the cap, a bragging right to other publishers and more importantly shareholders. Another side effect was that many of Activision's first-person shooters used id Software's technology (or idtech as everyone just calls it) for the majority of their games. id Software licences their tech, and if you have a nice long-term relationship they will cut you a deal.

This was not the main reason that id Software had more power than most devs in regards to the publisher relationship, but because they did not need the money. Milestones are the benchmark to measure a game's development progress but also the leash a publisher controls most devs. Activision did not even see Doom 3 until it was in Alpha. I don't mean that milestones were not discussed, but Activision did not even see code until id Software felt like they were good and ready in Alpha. Development had run months late from the original schedule but that did not matter. id Software also had total control over marketing, whether it was screenshots, videos, press tours, E3, anything that had to do with their games went through them for approval. I have never seen marketing people so close to tears than when trying to get six screenshots for a magazine cover or trying to get the box art finished. Marketing isn't used to that practice. id Software was very particular about everything, and Activision was fine with that long as the dev kept delivering.

There are a few developers like this out and guessing who is based on how big the games are. Basically if a developer is responsible for making a billion dollars of profit each time a game is shipped for a hot publisher, they tend to earn power back. By the way, I do not mean to imply that a developer is better than a publisher when steering the ship—I have seen the same types of mistakes made by both, and the dynamic shifts to something new and rather unusual.

The "Middlemen"

Over the last few years, I have been hired out as a consultant, kind of a Creative Director for hire to help projects during the initial creation, get on the right track, or by "fixing" when the process is not going well. What I actually end up doing for the majority of projects is work on site with the developer as the Creative Director, becoming a part of the team creating the game directly for months or even years at a time. I may be paid by the Publisher as a contractor but am embedded with whomever needs me, helping to lead the project and team. I really enjoy this "the man in the middle" relationship as I have no real allegiances to anyone beyond the game. Politics play a role in any company, big or small, dev or publisher, and I get to operate outside to some degree. Both "sides" know that I am here for the game only, I have no dog in this race. I will not be promoted, get a raise, or have my neck on the corporate line. I am not worrying about milestones or schedules directly, and have no quarterly report to prepare for executives. If I say something will make the game better, it comes exclusively from the viewpoint of making a better game. Functioning in this position is extremely liberating after decades of being in the industry. Take my advice and direction, or don't, but always know it comes from an impartial place focusing on making the game great.

At times the hard part is finding Developers who accept they may need help in the first place and don't have "that person" internally to fill the role (or the current person is performing poorly), and are willing to accept an outsider. Also, Publishers must accept that the project needs help, realize they don't have someone who can do the job, and be willing to pay an outsider to and fix any issues. This recognition takes a certain amount of enlightenment to self-assess and ask for help. I have been very lucky, and my previous work has alleviated a lot of the "outsider" worry. I don't talk about what makes a better game, I help developers and publishers make a better game and have the track record. Overall this is beneficial to everyone but is quite an odd relationship that I have not often seen in the games industry.

Non-centralised Development

Games are made all across the world by teams that may be located in different countries. Now with high speed internet and decent collaborative supporting software, non-centralised development is completely possible. This does not mean face-to-face meetings and sessions are not important. Skype is great, but for certain discussions sitting around a table with whiteboards and unlimited coffee is much better.

I try to remind myself face-to-face meetings are important when getting into a taxi in Moscow and as the door opens with pop house music blaring, and the driver says in broken English "Seatbelt? No, only weak people wear seatbelts". And I think "This is how every YouTube 'Russian drivers are crazy and crash' video starts... and this is how I die". By the way, those videos are 100% accurate, traffic laws in Russia are merely suggestions. If a vehicle will "fit" then it's a lane: sidewalks, ditches, whatever. Laws there were best described by Artplant's lead programmer while I was visiting. We were taking a break from a meeting, and he was going to have a smoke. On the plane ride over, we heard people complaining that Russia just passed a law banning smoking in workplaces. Walking about 10 feet to a staircase, he lights a cigarette. I ask, "Hey, we just talked about the new law passed about smoking indoors". In a thick Russian accent, he replies, "Laws? Heh, ya, Russia has a lot of laws", and then takes a long drag on his cigarette and continues to smoke. Russia is one of the coolest, most badass, and more scary places I have visited.

Artplant is a good example of non-centralised development. Head office is in Oslo, Norway, the bulk of programmers are in Tver, Russia, and other employees and contractors are scattered throughout Europe. I had a designer in Brighton, another in Istanbul, and the Development Director (schedule person) in Bristol. We lived in Skype and Google Docs, and made sure everyone commented commitments to the code and documents clearly. We worked in English, but for 98% of the team that was a second or third language. I myself am based in London but travelled to Oslo nearly every week to work. I could have easily spent more time working from home, but the majority of what I do is coordinating and having high level discussions with art directors, etc., and find it easier meeting in person. I am a bit old school in that respect. This kind of collaboration would not be possible ten, even five years ago, and I think this is the way forward in the industry.

What are the advantages of being an internal or external studio?

One of the major reasons independent studios sell to a publisher is stability. Being an independent studio means constantly chasing the next project, working for hire, and trying to keep the doors open in addition to making great games. When a publisher buys you, besides making a good amount of cash if things go well, the overhead becomes the publisher's problem. Not literally of course, but now the studio has partners working to ensure they remain healthy. Also, studios gain expertise and resources from being part of a larger "whole", and if leveraged correctly, can be a huge advantage. Access to tech, facilities, assets, and raw knowledge can be a real force multiplier for a studio.

Drawbacks include being one studio of possibly many. Most publishers are publicly traded and financial decisions are done on a macro level, and have quarterly numbers to meet. A studio may not be the top priority or almost as bad is being the top priority with an extreme amount of pressure to succeed. Also, a studio must learn to work within a larger organisation, play the politics, and otherwise understand how a multibillion dollar corporation works (or doesn't). Last week before the buyout, the biggest concern was making sure that "X" on the game was fun and working while signing up the sequel. Now this week after the buyout, there is a board meeting and another game missed certain targets so the publisher wants to move your ship date up, plus QA, a shared global resource across the publisher, has increasing burn rates so the game budget is now over, etc. Studios gain stability but also the stress and responsibility of managing overhead.

How the size of a developer impacts work and culture

There are many different team compositions, but I will try to describe the most common formats. These are broad categories, but I have been part of 20+ teams over the years, and experienced the changes and shifts when teams and companies hit transition points, along with noticing the differences, advantages, and disadvantages.

Single project companies

In is usually the first phase of a developer's scale, with 30 to 40 people involved. The team dynamic is very tight: everyone knows everyone else, communication is simple, and there are only a handful of managers that run the entire group. The Creative Director or whomever is steering the vision, often talking to everyone personally on a regular basis. Reviews, meetings, and other important syncing/communication events happen spontaneously and as content is created. The atmosphere tends to be less formal, and the whole team can turn on a dime by taking a new tack, and adding or even changing direction completely on the fly with relative ease.

The team is usually tight-knit and social, and feels much like hanging out with friends at times. Everyone is trying to accomplish the same goal, and the sense of teamwork is strongest when at this "phase" in my opinion. There are drawbacks— the biggest one is bandwidth. Shipping a AAA game on multiple platforms when resources are limited is difficult. Creating a game with 50 characters models while having one character modeller isn't possible. Most largescale games nowadays are made by teams far bigger than 40.

This brings me to a relatively new type of team/company—the single project with over 200 people. These only existed in the last decade or sowith the big publishers such as Ubisoft, Activision, and Electronic Arts. These teams are absolutely huge and work exclusively on AAA titles, requiring monumental amounts of content and a large enough team to get the content done in a reasonable amount of time. Large and rather unwieldy, these teams feel more like factories in certain ways than creative shops. This is not always true, but by compartmentalising not only work but communication and resources, people start to get the feeling of isolation. Keeping 200+ people "in the loop" is pretty much impossible. Add that teams of this size require far more layers of administration and management in general, you start to get divisions within divisions and people not knowing what exactly "that guy" does around here.

Multiple teams spread over multiple companies working on a single title

The problem with games having huge complexity and large amounts of content can also be solved by having multiple, separate teams.

This has several advantages:

1) Maintain smaller individual teams smaller and keeping those advantages.

2) Allow for teams to be in different locations—talent can be anywhere.

3) Certain teams and companies may specialise in particular areas which can maximise skillsets.

The downsides are present when maintaining communication between the different teams, as well having a solution if tech and assets are being shared, which is common. The first time I worked within team scenario was with the *Call of Duty* franchise. Early on we found that the expertise in multiplayer is a hard thing to master and may not be present in the same team creating the single-player game. Add in that the games were getting huge in scope and content, it just made sense to have the multiplayer completed by another studio. This has become a common scenario especially in games with both single-player and multiplayer aspects.

Single company, two teams

Generally this structure takes place after a company has some success with their first title and want to expand in order to spread some of the risk around, plus create more cool games. The studio takes on a second project with the full second team. This practice has the side effect of changing the dynamic and feel of a company significantly and is often underestimated. What starts is "us" and "them" as not everyone is working on the same project, leading to politics beyond the interpersonal in any team. One project will be going better than the other, closer to shipping, or some other aspect that requires more attention, resources, or any other element that is limited. One project will get closer to shipping and require "all hands on deck" to help out. This scenario has to be managed while making sure that the team identity is strong but not stronger than the company identity. Everyone is in the same boat, sinking or swimming together. When BioWare went from just having the *Baldur's Gate* team to adding the MDK2 team, we could feel the change. Ray and Greg (the owners of BioWare) did a good job of ensuring BioWare as a whole had team spirit, but there was some "What are they doing on the other side of the building?" feelings from that point onwards. This perception cannot be helped and is part of any growing company.

Single company, 3+ teams

This scenario is the extension and expansion of similar issues when moving from one to two teams. At this point, the team identity usually outweighs the company one from day-to-day. Forget about knowing everyone's names, people now work in an office of sorts. Add extra layers of management, managers to manage managers, and the whole feel of the company becomes more corporate. This is the start of "central resouces", which has different elements such as animation, tools, etc., become not attached to any project but as an independent team and entity with projects booking and scheduling their time and talent.

This practice is definitely more efficient in specific ways, especially as the demand for certain skills and resources ebbs and flows a great deal in a project depending on the phase, but reinforces the "us" and "them" aspect as teams are literally competing for resources within the same company. If one project finds itself late or in trouble, taking resources to solve their issues, another team can't help but feel some resentment. The real rathole is when that shift in focus then puts a project in jeopardy to become the problem project down the road. I have witnessed companies lurch from emergency to emergency for years because of this ongoing firefighting. Imagine being placed in a position where you do not control all the necessary resources and the situation is near impossible to schedule or predict. Not a good way to run a project, let alone a company.

When a company has 3+ projects, the feel of working there is the same whether it's an internal publisher with game development or an external independent developer. This is neither good nor bad, only that reaching a certain critical mass of people working together blurs the lines of who is doing what, and the culture tends to blend, becoming more formal and corporate. I have worked many times with small teams where there is no HR department with team building exercises consisting of nightly outings at the local pub. Big corporations or large developers could not exist without a person managing holidays, complaints, and team building. Team days out are some of the few times that some people will ever interact even if they are in the same building and their paycheques are signed by the same people.

No matter what the team size, internal or external, or even how many active projects, the overall feel and tone of the company will vary greatly. In general, how "good" a place is trickles down from the top.

So who pays for all this? How games get published

Games cost inane amounts of money to make these days, and with these high costs comes a lot of scrutiny in the decisions not only which game gets made, but every step along the way of any game's development. Every publisher has their own processes to help make these assessments and it involves many people on the project with a wide range of specialities to really get it right. If you are spending one hundred million dollars, you don't want to put it on a project solely because "bob says it will be good". That's just not enough.

Serious Sam

Within Activision in the early 2000s, we had a process call "Greenlight": a fantastic set of meetings where a project is reviewed at key checkpoints in its development cycle. The heads of every department discussed the project, which was either "green lit" to move forwards or "red lit" if there were issues (usually meant cancellation). This was a "do or die" type setup, even though very few projects were ever "red lit" and cancelled, and it goes without saying this process could be rather stressful.

I had just started working at Activision when a game using a codename was being pitched, and the studio making the game was looking for a publishing partner. The game was being created by Croteam using their own technology and was a light-hearted but gory first-person shooter. Croteam had worked on the game for a while and was currently at the prototype phase where parts could be played. Pitching to various publishers, they were looking for a partner to not only pay for the rest of the development but to publish, market, and sell it around the world. Since I had a design background, and I had just joined the "shooters" group, Activision management thought it would be a good idea for me to assess the game and shepherd it through the GL process as my first project for first-hand on how the Publisher did things. The game was early in its lifecycle, but I could easily see what Croteam could do on a technical level, and the design was very basic which was its intent from the start. A fun, brains off, action cranked up shooter. I wrote up a report on the important points, reviewed the schedule, and figured out if the remaining work was an accurate assessment. I talked to marketing regarding their thoughts, comparing the game not only to our own internal games being made but the competition.

They wrote up Profit and Loss estimates (P&Ls) with best- and worst-case numbers. We plugged in the costs to date and remaining expenses to get a full financial picture. After I talked to PR about their thoughts, where it fit into the release line-up, how they would promote it, etc. This is before we even had the Greenlight meeting. This process was a great way to learn how Activision operated.

The day of the Greenlight meeting I was a bit nervous. The VPs of all the departments and the president of the company attend to basically pass judgement whether or not a project should live or die. It's nearly as straight-forward as "thumbs up or thumbs down" but without the crowds jeering and slightly fewer people being fed to lions. My first formal meeting within the company, I had only been there for a few weeks and was the first time I met most of these people.

Production always spoke first as we were closest to the game development—if the game was not fun or had no chance of being done on time, we knew there was no point in talking any further. My Executive Producer did most of the talking (thankfully) until the specifics were needed about the design and the overall quality. I mentioned the game was fun but basic. Comparing it to our current games in development (which included *Wolfenstein*, *Star Wars: Jedi Knight*, etc.), it was technically simpler and less ambitious but fun for what it was. The team clearly knew what they were doing and making, and revelling in delivering. The cost for making the remainder of the game was very inexpensive compared to our other games, and the milestones seemed reasonable from the available information. These types of meetings are information gathering and collating sessions, so be honest and straightforward as possible since big decisions whether to fund a project or not are made. You want to be positive but not misleading. Optimistic but realistic. The president Ron Doornink actually walked-up to the PC showing off the game and played for a bit. I respect Ron always did that during my Greenlights, and as the senior executive he wasn't required but wanted to see for himself. Everyone seemed satisfied with my report and presentation, and were nodding in agreement.

Next up was Marketing, and we all turned to the printout pages with the P&L figures, which showed that Activision would have a small profit of a few hundred thousand dollars on the worst case and slightly more for the standard case. Ron asked a few pointed questions about game quality and what was the likelihood of pushing it further in a few aspects. I answered by reiterating my points before. "Well ok, I guess we should not move forward then, the bandwidth that this game would take in our group, QA, etc., just isn't worth it". And that was it—done and dead within Activision.

I was stunned. My first greenlight was a red light. I felt terrible. *Where did I screw up?* I was pulled aside by my EP when he saw the look on my face after the meeting. "Look, Activision is a huge company with dozens of games being made. Each one takes up resources. Whether they are successful or not, we can only make so many games at a time. A profit of a few hundred K is just not worth our time when we could be spending the same amount or resources ensuring a larger game's success or starting one that had more potential".

There was nothing wrong with the game, but when considering what could be made is very different from deciding what should be made. I had never considered what a large company's priorities should be and factors they worried about. My whole career up until that point centred around one project at a time: *one game, my game*. This experience was a real eye-opener and changed how I looked at development. I am so glad my manager talked with me and set me straight, but it did not stop some teasing by my co-workers: "Jeeze, only been here a few weeks and you cancelled a game". The game eventually became *Serious Sam*, a successful franchise that continues to this day with a VR version coming out later this year that looks great. Do I think Activision made a mistake? No, not at that time nor now. The game was not right for Activision, but I am very glad it continued development and found a home with another publisher, and was bought and played by so many over the years.

Baldur's Gate II: Shadows of Amn

The other end of the spectrum is a full sequel based on a successful previous game. *Baldur's Gate* was released in 1998 and the first big title for BioWare and myself. We enjoyed phenomenal success even though it was in a genre that was close to dead at the time (RPG). Based on the quick success, Interplay decided BioWare should create a sequel. The meeting happened quite soon afterwards, and we first made the expansion pack *Baldur's Gate: Tales of the Sword Coast* to bridge the two games, add in a few features, fix bugs, and generally improve the game. During the development of the expansion, the green light was given to make a full sequel with planning and development overlapping both projects.

The best part about working on a sequel, if you are not reinventing the tech, is taking advantage of 100% what was learned from the previous game. What tools work, what didn't. What types of quests were fun, which were... let's say less so. The engine will have matured and bugs ironed out, and the programming team can focus nearly exclusively on making the game better rather than trying to get anything to work. This foundation allows the studio to do everything they wished could have been done the first time around but were either too inexperienced, the tech was still changing, and most likely they ran out of time. An added benefit is from nearly day one the game being made can be played and viewed rather than waiting months for tech to set up., Almost from the start the game is fun.

Another advantage is making accurate estimates on the time needed for development. You know a map will take three weeks to make as by the end of the last game the average time for an interior was three weeks consistently. This means you can make things with a confidence that it won't be cut due to time, and spend any extra time purely polishing the content instead of scrambling just to keep everything from falling over.

Lastly it is a great opportunity to add features that the previous game did not have time for. In *Baldur's Gate* the UI took up a lot of space, and experienced players did not need it all the time which took away from looking at the pretty (for the time) game world. In *Baldur's Gate II: Shadows of Amn* we provided the option where the UI slid off to the sides, and players could invoke it when needed with a press of a button or pausing the game to make gameplay decisions. We always wanted this function from the start of the first game but did not have the time to implement properly. The UI programmer had too many tasks to make the game work, let alone implement this "quality of life" feature. In *BGII*, however, since the backbone for everything already worked, he spent the time to implement this function, and from a UI perspective, this is one of my favourite changes from *BGI* to *BGII*. I can't play the original anymore without it. In fact *Beamdog* remade the game recently and included the sliding UI feature in the original game (and made *BGI* for iOS which is plain awesome).

Basically sequels let you atone for any sins in the original, and it is refreshing being able to make NEW mistakes instead of living with the old ones.

I have been fortunate enough to make games from both the publishing and development point of view. The first seven or so years of my career I worked as a designer and a producer for developers such as BioWare and Relic . I did everything including interfacing with the Publisher's producer, marketing, and PR, and getting projects ready to pitch at publishers for consideration. Then I worked for eight years at publishers at Activision doing the flip side of my previous jobs, and served as part of the due diligence for many games pitched to our company. Most recently I have been a creative and design director, and a consultant straddling the line between the two roles through my own company Forerunner. Often hired by the

Publisher I work onsite as a developer with the studio team to help make a better game. Next I will focus on the development of "traditional" PC and console AAA games as they tend to have the most nuanced and varied paths into existence.

The AAA game: Assessing the risks

The relationship between developers and publishers vary a great deal, depending on the circumstances, and since every project is different, there is unlimited room for differing "flavours" of relationships. Bottom line for most relationships is that the publisher fronts the money for the developer to create the game. Ignoring all the variables such as royalty percentages, marketing budgets and internal costs, publishers want to minimize risks. The costs of games are spiralling, nearly out of control. We spent more on QA for a project in 2013 than the ENTIRE development budget for *Baldur's Gate I*, which shipped in 1998. That's a three year project with 50+ staff hired by the end. Spending 10 to 15 million dollars on development is about average for a console or PC game a few years ago (in the early 2000s) and does not count costs such as QA, marketing, PR, manufacturing, audio, and software licenses. Now the really big titles (think *Call of Duty*) played on console or PC have budgets of 50 to 100+ million dollars or more. These budges are crazy and expensive, and publishers want to minimize the risk when huge sums of money are spent on making a game.

The Risks:

There are three major risks that can make or break a game pitch to a publisher. That's not entirely true—there are hundreds but three major "check boxes" stand out that a publisher worries about:

- Team
- Technology
- Intellectual Property

These risks have different weightings based on the project being pitched, but if any one of these legs in the "tripod" is weak, it is an instant red flag for the people performing the due diligence on the proposal. I will explore the importance of each major risk along with several other risks important to someone auditing a game pitch.

Team: When a publisher is looking at a new project, the team is one of the key risks in the "tripod". What has this team done before? Who are its key members? Have they worked on a game before like the one proposed? How organized is the team? These are all valid concerns that a publisher looks to have answered before moving forward. These are a few hints of questions you should have answers for and develop an overall plan before pitching a project. Include a listing of your entire team so far, including people still needed to be hired for the scope of the project. The listing of the people already involved should list all their credits, and what they bring to the team and role.

Game Design: Sounds simple, but it's not. The design document should include everything from the core design, UI mock-ups[1] to control schemes [2]. Without a well fleshed out game design, there is no possibility for creating a staffing plan or a schedule. These are all interdependent and need careful consideration.

---

[1] How the user interface (UI) will look on the screen to the user.
[2] Shows how the user will interact with the game: which keys, buttons, or controllers the player will use and how each will work.

153

Schedule: A rough schedule must list the development plan for the remainder of the project with a high detailed pass on the concept to first playable milestones[3]. This shows the publisher that you have considered the project as a whole, and understand the scope and scale of the game. This is possibly the most difficult requirement as there are many unknowns and requires a decent design doc, staffing plan, and deep understanding on the requirements involved.

Technology: Due to the nature of the industry, technology moves exceedingly fast. New features in graphics, design, and gameplay happen constantly, and saying your game will have all the "bells and whistles" just won't do. The absolutely best way to convince a publisher that there is a low technology risk is having a prototype up and running showing the high risk (read: new) features that the game intends to have. Without a good design up front, this is impossible.

Prototype: Get a prototype up and running soon as possible before pitching the game to any potential publishers. The demo does not have to be perfect with 60 frames per second[4] and all the gameplay

---

[3] A project is often very large, so it is broken down into measurable checkpoints or units of work called milestones.

elements, but it does have to prove the concept and address the high risk areas. Saying the game can support 2,000 players in multiplayer will not be trusted unless you have some sort of demonstrable proof. All decent publishers have a due diligence group that have tech, art, and design people involved, so faking them out is not an option; however, you can convince these experts on a technical level by demoing a prototype and discussing the technology, focusing specifically on the solutions to the unique challenges that the project faces.

Licences:

Another way to help reduce risk on a project is to licence technology, which can be through the use of middleware [5] renderers, multiplayer SDKs[6], or an entire engine depending on the needs and staff skillsets. Proving knowledge and experience with the tech, and

---

[4] 60 frames per second (FPS) is considered the bare minimum by some gamers for a final game performance, although 30 FPS is fairly common on console games. Lower frame rates in games with lots of action can look "jerky". TV and Movies are 24 FPS for comparison.

[5] Middleware is software that bridge gaps between different aspects of a game. A physics engine could be middleware as an example. Not a full engine but parts.

[6] SDK is short for Software Development Kit. Essentially a self contained feature or set of features that you can use "as is" once included into your own code.

you're the licensed technology can handle the scope it is required. Whether it is CRYENGINE® 3 or Unity [7], make sure that the tech is relevant and understood. Publishers have many intelligent and skilled people who cannot be fooled, and your pitch will be dissected down to its smallest components.

Intellectual Property: Intellectual property (IP) is a buzzword in the industry. When people lament the lack of creativity in games, they mean in the IP more often than not. Publishers want lower risk, and a known IP such as a movie property, summer blockbuster, game sequel, or sports league has instant name recognition with the general populace (and most likely their target audience as well). This last leg in the tripod is one of the most difficult. As a developer, creating your own IP is challenging. Several successful games must be released to demonstrate a proven track record along with the other two legs of the tripod before a publisher considers a developer good enough that the risk is lessened.

---

[7] These engines and many others offer all the components needed to create the foundations for a full game with little to no middleware required.

156

Publishers often have an IP and tech ready, and are looking for a competent developer to deliver the game. This happens more than you would think, and the developer must have a proven track record to be considered.

"Hey, I have a great idea!": Where new projects come from

"Hey I have this great idea for a game".

The number of times I have heard this from casual acquaintances to someone I just met at a party or social situation when they learn what I do for a living is shocking. This is probably the most common thing I hear besides the question "How do you get into the games industry?" This is often followed by a hushed tone and then "But I am not sure I should tell you—it's a million dollar idea and I don't want to give it away".

First of all, no it's not a million dollar idea and certainly not by itself. I am not being flippant or glib, but the "good ideas" are actually the easiest part assuming someone knows what a good idea is or looks like. When starting to make a game, we are leading a target—determining what will be fun and popular months or even years in the future. The ability to identify tech, game design, and even platform and monetisation shifts that will happen between

"Hey, I have this great idea" and becoming available to the players. A super high level concept of "a game where 'X' does 'Y'" is all but meaningless. Also funny is how often the game idea involves the speaker's life or job... or super niche. No, a game about managing supply lines in the American Civil war will not have mass appeal—sorry. I know you work in a warehouse and participate in 1860s re-enactment weekends, and it can be super interesting, but most people in the world would not care to play this as a game.

Making a successful game is nearly all in the execution, not the high level idea. The thousands of design, tech, and artistic decisions that actually make the game are what matters. Any popular game can be distilled into a few lines of description that says nothing about its fun or quality. It's called an elevator pitch (a pitch given to someone in the time it takes to ride in an elevator). This is what most people give as their "game idea". Don't get me wrong, this is required for any good game, but by itself it's worthless. "It's a game where you are a super soldier, and you have to work with other players online to achieve mission objectives. You get to choose your weapons and upgrade skills and gear as you progress". What game is that? This could be a game from the *Call of Duty* or *Battlefield* series, or just about any first-person shooter from the last ten years. Throw in the words sci-fi, post-apocalyptic, or gritty realistic, and you have seriously covered 90% of them. It is also a great idea since the first-person shooter genre has made billions of dollars, but those two sentences have very little to do with the success. So if great game ideas don't come from the street, where do they actually start?

There are several ways that a project gets started and varies based on platform and cost. This process is more of a tree than a straight line with these as the major routes for making AAA games:

- Wholly new game
    - Publisher has an IP/franchise they want to develop, so they pitch to developers.
    - IP/franchise holder has a game they want to make, so they pitch to publishers.
    - Developer has a game they want to make, so they pitch to publishers.
    - Identified open space in the market. A completely new game is the rarest of new project origins. This can be conceived by publishers or developers, but it's usually developers. Wholly new concepts like Minecraft, or Katamari Damacy are fundamentally new and stand on their own as fresh concepts for a game
- Non-original creation

- Publisher wants to make a new game based on the success of a previous title, so pitches to developers.
- Fast follow[1] another game made by someone else to take advantage of what is currently popular, usually a publisher pitches to developers.

Nothing terribly shocking on this shortlist covering the vast majority of reasons games are pitched.

Now this does not take into consideration smaller productions or projects, also known as indie (short for independent) development. Self-funded, five people working in a basement can make whatever they please and do. This is where quirky and weird niche projects come to life. Some of these are the most fun you will have making or playing in the gaming world, but for every one of these great experiences, there will be 100 that die before they even ship, and the next 100 will never be played by anyone besides the makers and their family/friends. This could be for a host of reasons from lack of

---

[1] Fast follow means a game made very quickly in months, not years, and in general are frowned on by gamers as "Me too!" or knock offs. These can still be good games and make a lot of money.

polish or fun to simply lack of visibility because marketing a game is expensive and hard to do right.

Realistically and statistically most developers will not make money doing this unless they are the exception; however, succeeding can lead to great benefits aside from instant financial success, such as getting noticed by a larger group, enabling a relationship with a publisher or developer, and being able to take ideas further with some support. Also, this could be a big plus to your resume if searching for a long-term career in the games industry. I am not saying don't try—I would never say that—but be somewhat realistic about the industry. For every indie title like *Minecraft* with its incredible success, there are literally thousands of... um.... what was that game? Exactly! Names of games you cannot remember or have never played.

The life cycle of a AAA game: Putting it all together

There are a few legends in the games industry surrounding particular games that were difficult to create and ship. The most famous one is probably *Duke Nukem Forever*. The original game, *Duke Nukem*, was released in 1996 and was a great success. The sequel was started shortly afterwards but was not released until 2011. Now a standard games development cycle takes anywhere from 18 to 24 months, sometimes more, sometimes less. When entering your second decade of development, you know serious things had gone wrong, mostly likely often and repeatedly. As someone working in the industry, I would hear bits and pieces on what was happening behind the scenes from people working on the game or had left the various parties still working on it. The team changed technology several times requiring total restarts, changed direction or design with more restarts, added things, changed features, and generally "cocked it up". No single decision or person is really to blame, only a series of smaller bad choices made in a row, and peppered with a few bouts of insanity that made development worse. I did not work directly on that game, but come on... I shipped fifteen games in the time they completed one, and clearly it was an incredibly flawed process. So what is the proper process to make a game? What does the plan look like when it works?

Relationship between publishers and developers

A relationship between a publisher and a developer can vary greatly, with power and control over what games get made and when they ship in the hands of who is paying. This is the roughest of summaries. The standard relationship in AAA PC and console game making, however, is that a publisher pays a developer to create and maintain a game when specific milestones are delivered, spread throughout the development of the title. The amounts can range from a few hundred thousand dollars for a mobile title to over 100 million dollars for the larger, more familiar games.

Breakdown of the money spent:
- Licensing of intellectual property
- Licensing of tech/engines outside of the developer, including servers and other hosting and maintenance.
- Marketing

- Public relations (press, trade shows)
- Internal publishing costs, producers and other support
- QA
- Audio
- Payments to the developer over the duration of the game's creation, which is referred to as milestones

What is a milestone?

A milestone is a unit of measurement used within a schedule to quantify progress in creating a game. These "gates" are key for understanding the progress of the game development to determine whether it is going to plan, and are only paid on the successful completion of these milestones as judged by the publisher. You can tell why some developers are not huge fans of this set-up since the power resides with the publisher.

Milestones are usually defined by QA along with the developer and publisher before starting the project with some "wiggle room" for adjustments and iterative design in the early phases of creation to account for learning. These payments often are the only things keeping the doors open at a developer, and stating milestones are important is a rather understated sentiment.

What does it actually take to create a game?

Each project is different, having its own challenges and unique issues. To describe a proper project arc I will use a broad example, including actual elements within the sample outline I have experienced in projects that shipped. These important definitions are usually created by the publisher QA who signs off on the later stages of the game such as Alpha, Beta and Final. When a game has gone successfully passed a phase, it is a big deal with many ramifications.

Many "triggers" are pulled at Alpha for instance. QA gets added en masse to the project, and documenting bugs starts to flow into the databases. Adjusting the game can begin in earnest as no major shifts in features beyond fixing and balancing remain. Marketing also can feel far more confident on dates and their campaigns as this milestone is met. Every major milestone is about limiting risk, assessing progress, and defining how resources should be spent moving forward. There are several key phases in this process.

Concept Phase: One to three months

The concept phase in most projects lasts a –one to three months with only a skeleton crew working on the game at this point. The leads are involved with brainstorming around a specific idea, working out key features, defining style, and identifying any risks that need to be addressed for the prototype phase. At the end of this process, the following should be available:

- Game design document
- Technical design document
- Art style guide
- Rough schedule showing manpower hours needed to make the game
- Goals for the prototype
- List of outstanding risks

Prototype Phase: One to three months

This phase checks assumptions in the concept phase for the first time:

- Does the high concept still make sense?
- At least on paper, has each risk from the technical design document been addressed.
- Does the prototype contain all the key features, and do they work?
- Did the schedule for the creation of the prototype hold up? Was it accurate?

There are warning flags at this stage: the prototype was very late, key elements to the core design proving that the game was fun/unique did not get completed, or the game play was not fun. This is far harder to assess than you would imagine since much of the code is hacked together[1], the art is rudimentary, there is no game play balance, and the prototype is usually a single level or even room call. Experience is needed to see through the rough edges and focus on the real issues. Anything that is not addressed in the build needs to be addressed in documentation, outstanding design, technical details, and architecture, plus everything from character design to UI flow. Once this stage has been passed, the game goes into full production and all the "blanks" need to be filled in before hiring dozens, if not hundreds, of people when the project is in full swing.

This phase is sometimes called "first playable", and in most ways is more descriptive. The biggest caveat is that the whole game is not playable, but the core concepts are understood and any risks have their final assessment attached. In theory, there are no new surprises after this stage and every outstanding question is answered.

Production Phase: –Ten to twelve months

---

[1] "Hacked together" as in creating throwaway code and other assets to complete the phase fast as possible, not necessarily in the best or most optimised way.

The production phase is the time spent between prototype or first playable and the period in which the title is declared Alpha. The bulk of the content and features going into the game are created. Each title's production phase varies a great deal depending on scope and scale of the project, and is when the team needs to be at maximum capacity. Planning and designing ahead of time pays off during this phase, or if done poorly comes back to haunt you. There are usually milestone payments from the Publisher spread out over this time period based around major features being delivered. Passing or failing milestones during this rather long phase is one of the few metrics deducing the health of the schedule and risk to the delivery dates.

Alpha Phase: Three months

The simplest definition of Alpha is that all features are complete, whether a gameplay, graphical, or other supporting code feature. Each level exists and is playable, every asset is represented, UI is available, every key part of the game is ready. There will be assets that continue to be worked on and art swapped in/out, but the overall scope of the game is now locked. Except for designating the Final phase, this is the most important milestone a project goes through.

Since all features are now implemented, optimisations can begin from the art and coding team. Total memory usage and other metrics are now accurate as there is far less flux in features and content compared to the main production of the previous phase.

QA begins in earnest now that the features can be properly reviewed and are considered complete. The bug database grows from this point onwards as any previous QA reviews would have had huge caveats, including whole sections of the game marked by development as "please don't write anything up on this section yet". At Alpha all bets are off, and QA performs a proper and full-scale review of the whole game.

All features, gameplay. and code are determined as locked, but this is phase requirement that gets violated most often and the reason why Alpha and Beta phases sometimes "blend" together. A feature runs late but is deemed low risk that Alpha should be called by QA so the rest of the process can start. This feature takes weeks or even longer with "real" Alpha not occurring until that feature is officially completed.

Art is locked down, and no major assets should be changed beyond optimisations and fixes due to bugs. Balance and optimisation of features and assets cannot really happen until the art stops changing. Team members submit code, features, and assets many times a day which can change performance greatly. These submissions have to level off before completing any real optimisation work.

Balance becomes the focus of the design team. Now that the features are in and the levels (or whatever is relevant to the game genre) are playable, it is time to make the game "fun". Going into Alpha, every single game has major issues that get in the way of fun. The final months of the game are so important to quality and fun, and becomes a real shame if the game is running late since this part of development suffers. Nearly every game that has flopped made this mistake and was victim of cutting short the "Alpha to ship" times.

Beta Phase: One month

Beta is mainly locking down content. All assets and changes to the game are done. Only major bugs are addressed moving forward and defined as those that prevent shipping the game. Balance is done, art is complete, and people are being locked out of committing code and assets to help reduce the chance of introducing new bugs. The bug database should be down to a few hundred bugs at most, and great care and attention is maintained whenever anyone touches anything. You can't afford to be adding bugs and issues at this stage due to mistakes or sloppy commits of code or assets.

Final Steps: Two to four weeks

Depending on the publisher and the project, the next steps generally occur in this order:

QA approves the build for a "pre-submission" to first parties, such as Microsoft and Sony[2]. This is a friendly "heads up" with code sent over for the console manufacturers to play and document their own bugs before the game is "officially" submitted for review and release. This resembles getting the answers before taking the test but saves time for everyone, and a game cannot be released without passing the checklists of these manufacturers.

After receiving bugs from the pre-sub, development fixes them and hopefully aligns with QA calling "code release" of the game internally at the Publisher. This means the bug database is zeroed out. Realistically what happened is that there are no more "A" bugs, and anything else of worth in the database has been put into a "for

---

[2] First parties "own" the hardware and include Microsoft, Sony and Nintendo. Second parties are the developers who make the games for those hardware platforms and independent from first parties. Both first and second parties can make games, however.

patch" folder. The builds are sent to Sony and Microsoft for them to review officially and sign off, and then the game is ready for manufacturing.

Now that games ship globally, localizations must be code released on the same day as the "main" English version (and are often found on the same physical disk). A broken Czech menu can actually hold up a worldwide release of a multimillion dollar game. The last few bugs are always a pain and risk. Every time the code is opened for a fix, you risk adding a new bug. Taking into account the turnaround time, this ends up being a nerve-wracking few weeks: fix a bug, make a build, test the build at the developer, test it at the publisher, send it to first party to test... wait for the e-mail or phone call to see if it passes, and repeat if not fixed or something new pops up. The entire team is on call, and any expected 2 a.m. phone call during a project will be during this time as every minute counts.

Alpha tests/Beta tests: A new facet

Although the concept of public Alpha/Beta tests are not new, this practice is slowly morphing into different tangents from when they started. First let's go over these tests and how they are used.

In general, having an advanced, public facing Alpha or Beta available is for testing out key components of usually online features. They are limited in scope and duration, and are accessible before the actual release of the game to sort out any issues. Someone may ask what is the reason for the tests since the developers have QA? The answer is yes, but QA would never catch these issues that the public tests highlight. Developers cannot test every public router or hardware configuration, or even accurately determine "what happens if 50,000 people simultaneously try to matchmake at the same time" with an onsite QA team. Testing these items means that when the game goes live the team knows that everything should work. If a game has an online component of any kind, I would strongly recommend having some sort of public test before launch. The complexity of both features and backbone components to make them work together have increased so much, involve many moving parts in the code, and with third party services, locations, and people, the odds something goes wrong is 100%. Fix it before launch. People on Alpha/Beta expect problems while paying customers buying released games do not and nor should they.

Marketing views anything released to the public as a chance for people to get a sneak peek and the public will make assumptions as well as talk very loudly and verbosely on message boards about their experiences in the early access. . Marketing fears nothing more than bad experiences or some sort of backlash from releasing a game that is subpar. Since the game is often pre-Alpha at the timing of these tests, much of the game is unfinished, unfun, and downright ugly. The influence of marketing is that we end up spending far more time polishing parts of the game that would not normally get attention to have a more complete experience. This continues blurring the lines as players see what appears to be a polished and "final" game. The developers just want to test if their online matchmaking code works, but end up spending time on a weapon sound effect, a wall texture, or balancing a mechanic that is still a first pass. This influence pushes back the date for the Alpha test later, making the testing less useful as there is limited time to address any issues that do come up.

Another problem is that people, including within the industry or even the team, see these prelaunch tests as meant for varying reasons and have different expectations. Broadly speaking they can be defined as follows:

- *Alpha Test:* Sometimes called a tech demo. The purpose is testing core features of the game many months in advance of release as possible to ensure these work. Usually very limited access and offered to a small number of public participants.

- *Beta Test:* Last minute feedback of balance and testing features under "load". Usually done much later in the process and open to far more participants, often getting confused as the Demo. In some respects, Beta fills much of the role a Demo performs. The greater player headcounts mean a larger impact of opinion, so Beta is a more polished example of code than the Alpha test.
- *Demo:* This test uses final game code and serves as a marketing tool exclusively. The Demo is released four to six weeks before the game hits the shelves, and any problems that arise can only be addressed in a patch since the game has been sent to final certification and the manufacture. Demos used to be a big deal and were common, but more likely now is a "free weekend" where people can download the entire game and play for a short period of time. Creating demos is a lot of work and an entire release cycle (with their own Alphas, Betas, and submissions) which are expensive and time consuming.

The last step: Shipping

Call of Duty: Finest Hour was a very painful shipping experience as I described earlier. I could write a whole book about the insanity of the game production, but let me tell you how its impact extended beyond the normal work expectation. I was working at Activision at the time as a Producer/Creative Director in the UK. The multiplayer part of the game was being made by Kuju based outside London. I was there to help with the design and shepherd the game as a producer. The experience had been a long process, but my part was finally done. Now I had not been back home to visit my family in Canada for over a year because of the game, and I needed to rectify that problem. My dad loves going to Las Vegas once a year and invited me to meet him there for a few days. I looked at the ship date of my game, added a few days, and agreed to meet him. As a Publishing Producer/Creative Director only on the multiplayer section, my work would be done when the development team submitted the code to first party sign-offs weeks before. Activision had enough Producers to handle anything that may come up, mainly being logistics and emergency bug fixing if anything happened at all, which would not involve me or my part could be solved over the phone/email with a simple "Yes, we need to fix that" or "No, we don't". I don't do any of the actual fixing but decide what should be and how regarding the game. I requested the holiday days in the schedule and received approval before booking my flights and hotels.

It's a long flight to Vegas from London, and add in time zone changes, anyone is wiped out when they land. I met my father for dinner and ate way too much prime rib... because I could. Free refills on prime rib? Yes please! Due to the jetlag, I was overtired and could not sleep so we decided to gamble a little and catch up for a few hours until the tiredness would take over. After such a hellish project, this vacation was exactly what I needed.

What I did know at the time was that the submission to Sony was not going well to put it mildly. The multiplayer part had been bounced back a few times from Sony QA for issues, and development was running out of time. Activision bought advertising space and shelf space, and spent a ton of money that revolved around guaranteeing that the game shipped on schedule.

This is when I get a phone call from my executive producer who was based in Los Angeles. "So, how are things?" I asked, knowing full well he would never phone me unless things were awful. He said, "So, our submission bounced again out of Sony" followed by a small pause on the phone. Tentatively I asked,"So, is there anything you can do to make sure, like to the point you are POSITIVE that the next submission will pass?". Another pause before he continued. "If we fail the next one, that's it—we miss our ship date and all that entails." Another few seconds of silence. "I will check on next flights back," I said. Explaining the situation to my dad as best I could, I could tell he was disappointed (so was I). Taking the next flight, I landed in London the following day. I spent more time flying to and from than actually in Vegas.

I went straight to the Developer, who was about to wrap up the build. We double- and triple-checked every outstanding and fixed bug before submitting another build to Sony. It passed.

To be fair, Activision reimbursed me, but I definitely "took one for the team". I could have said no, and nowadays I probably would have, but after crunching for so long with many people depending on it going well, for the game to fail at the last hour would have been crushing to everyone, myself included. Did having me go back make a difference? Not one bit, but it could have if things went sideways.

Now I go back home to Canada and go fishing every summer with my father, no matter what situation. The date may shift a few weeks here and there based on projects, but that time is taken regardless.

Activision spared nothing to ensure their games delivered on promised dates. *Call of Duty 2: Big Red One* was also running to the wire, . getting to a point where there was not enough time to even courier the final disks to Sony in Liverpool (where the final testing and sign-off for Europe happens). We decided the only way to make it in time was to send a producer with the disks on the next plane to Manchester and then drive west to Liverpool. This only saved a few hours, but the disks had to be at Sony's front desk for 8 a.m. with those few hours making the difference between shipping on time or not.

I received another late night phone call. The situation was explained to me: "So, the producer will be landing in Manchester tomorrow morning, and we need to guarantee she gets to Sony on time". I didn't say "I don't work on this title", "Surely she can take a cab or rent a car", or anything else. I knew this team and the effort they put in, and if I could help in any way, I would. I left immediately to Manchester from London (a few hours' drive) and checked into a weird little "hotel" at the edge of town, near the airport. Lalie Fisher (the Activision producer) would be landing on the first flight from LA with disks in hand at 6:30 a.m., and it was a 90 or so minute drive to Liverpool. Add that we would be in rush hour with all bets off whether we could make it. She landed at the airport on time, and we drove straight to Liverpool like a bat out of hell, arriving just in time for the Sony office to open at 8 a.m. I handed the receptionist a small package of disks and waited until the Sony QA manager came up to the front and took them. It was done. This little adventure felt more like dropping the one ring off at

Mordor. I turned around and drove her straight back to the airport so Lalie could fly back on the 11 hour return flight. With 22 hours of flying, she saw the airport, motorway, Sony front doors, and a McDonald's drive-through— Lalie's magical tour of England!

Examples of failing within the process

Here is an overview of areas where projects tend to fail as they go through the process of making games, including how it affects either meeting their release date or quality potential. With the flow of a project going from Concept - Prototype - Production - Alpha - Beta -Release, any issues or problems that occurred "upstream" corrupts everything downstream. Screw up in the concept phase and everything afterwards is hindered.

Problem: Poorly defined scope in Concept Phase.

Result: Game runs late or is impossible to complete.

How it happened: Not creating thorough concepts has a long lasting and trickledown effect on the whole project. Without enough detail, an accurate prototype cannot be created which is supposed to work out the risks, scope, and whether the idea is a good one or not. If the scope is wrong, there will be inaccuracies in either the schedule or people needed to make the game. If the risks are not all highlighted, development can find a major problem mid production needing to be solved that "just appeared" because they did not know to look for it. The worst outcome from not looking at the whole picture when creating the concept is that the idea, hard work, and millions of dollars spent results in creating a game that is not even fun. To fix this issue, developers often introduce new features mid-stream or at the end of the project, again costing more money and time.

Problem: Ignoring first playable results and moving ahead.

Result: Game runs late and/or when completed is not good, fun or even playable.

How it happened: This occurred when they failed first playable, and I don't mean the actual act of failing first playable where things often go wrong. If you fail this stage assess what went wrong, rework it, and try again—then it is a win. Failure is a step in the process often required to make great things. There is a whole development mindset used most often in mobile games built around "failing fast" where you generate many small concepts or prototypes and see what works, and quickly kill the ones that don't work. The far worse option is to create a first playable, fail, and continue forward regardless with the idea to "fix it as we go along". If the concept cannot be proved out then it is flawed and needs to be reworked. Greenlighting a whole project around having a "cool idea" or intellectual property without proving you can make a fun game is a fool's errand. Not sure why people think moving into full production with a fully ramped up team will fix anything other than doubling down the bet of pulling off the project before time or money runs out.

Knowing gamers: It's a big, big gaming world out there

Making games globally

My experience in Germany is a perfect and long-standing example. We were working on a game called *Wolfenstein*, a first-person shooter that took place during World War II and involved Nazi's, the occult, and well, more Nazis. Not a particularly historically accurate game, I'm sure the Nazis did not harness steampunk-like technology and demons to take on the Allies. One day as we were working on some aspect of the art, Kevin Cloud the Art/Creative Director at id Software casually mentioned "Hey, did you know that we (John Carmack, John Romero, etc.) *technically* have arrest warrants in Germany from making the last *Wolfenstein* game?" What?! "Ya, we used banned symbols like swastikas in the game as well as referenced Hitler and other things that the German government definitely frowns upon. I wonder if you guys will be added to the list of warrants too once this game is released.". Holy crap, I had no idea I was risking an international ban and possible arrest for making a game! Now this was years ago, and surely not really a thing that was enforced, especially since later there was a censored version released of the original (and we released a "safer" version of our game). But you can bet afterwards I was nervous (in a butt-clenching sort of way) at the border the next time I went to Germany for a press tour.

Germany's violence laws are very strict and constantly changing. What is acceptable one year may not be another. Even from title to title it can seem arbitrary. The country has banned symbols like swastikas, certain flags, and references to outlawed political and ideological groups. Try creating a WWII real-time strategy or first-person shooter game that has no violence or reference to Nazis, Hitler, or any flags or symbols for Germany from about 1928 to 1946. Now you see some of the issues that we overcame to get a game into some countries. This is not limited to Germany (who are some of the biggest gamers in the world, FPSs and RPGs especially). When localizing into Chinese, developers cannot mention anything about Taiwan or vice versa. Game creators must be sensitive to not only what is socially acceptable in their own country but aware of making changes for other countries that the game is destined for shipping. For multiplayer games in Korea,

Korean publishers/distributers and gamers want to see only Korean servers and don't want outsiders (non-Korean players) to see these servers. Why? No idea, but this is a requirement for shipping games to Korea. Does your game show the Communist Party in anything other than a positive light? If "no", forget China. Of course, if you do show the party in a positive light, the game is banned in other countries. It is a cultural minefield, and game makers cannot please all the people but must still be aware.

When creating games, publishers and developers alike want to target as many people possible. Achieving this goal means targeting to have the lowest system requirements (supporting older computers and hardware), the lowest age rating, the easiest learning curve to play the game, and available in as many territories as possible.

Translating games into as many languages possible makes perfect sense so that people from around the world can play;. however, this is not that easy. There are multiple levels of localization (fancy term meaning to translate): localizing the box and documentation, translating the in-game text, or pulling out all the stops with localizing the whole product—box, docs, text, and voice over. What decides which level of localization is going to be used for a particular project is simple—money.

For every localization, publishers need to pay for translating the text, support from the game makers to include the language, new packaging, manufacturing, and testing each language. This is not cheap. Some territories, China or Russia for instance, generally sell games for very cheap as they have to compete with grey market, and out-and-out piracy. For each copy sold only a few dollars are made, and this makes it very hard to justify localizing into certain territories, which of course just encourages more grey market. Not the best cycle to be in.

Even when a territory has a larger profit margin and can further entice localization with historically strong sales, there are other concerns. A country's local laws, regulations, and customs can force making even more changes to a title before shipping to their local stores.

Targeting specific gamers fallacy

Let's start with the whole discussion of "girl" games and girl gamers. Undeniably there are games made specifically targeting girls based on subject matter, but these have very little to do with the rise of gamers that are female. What girl gamers want is exactly the same as boy gamers—good games.

Making games for girls, older people, or any other group is a red herring as a goal. Start by making a good game. Those demographics are playing because someone made a good game that does not offend those groups with poor/stereotyping content, design, or execution. Think Pokemon is made for girls? No. So many play because it's a good game that allows anyone to play, identify with, and enjoy the content. The most likely outcome for chasing creating "a game for girls" is reinforcing bad stereotypes.

Subject matter does matter. Manly man with big guns shooting everything and swearing at his enemies does tend to appeal to mostly 13 to 24 year old males and ostracises huge swaths of potential gamers. You start to observe big swings in demographics when making games that more people identify with the protagonist. Massively Multiplayer Online Role-Playing Games (MMORPGs, or just. MMOs) games allow players to make many types of characters to play, customizing how the character looks and selecting either male and female. These games have female players accounting for over 50% of the gamers. The actual gameplay is just as "hack and slash" as many other games, but the subject matter, specifically the protagonist, is more flexible and appeals to many more players. These games also tend to highlight other aspects of gaming beyond combat. From social, crafting, to fishing and trade, players can progress in the world and have status by doing many types of gameplay. This approach appeals to a much wider type of person whether it's gender or even amount of time they can set aside to game during a given week. There will always be "men with big guns" or "kidnapped princess" tropes, but these games have seriously limited appeal with game makers being aware.

My point is that if you start with anything except "make a good game" as your first step, you are not going to create anything that will be successful in any market or with any audience.

Trolls, the community, and trying to make good things

Vampiric Sword and Golden Pantaloons:

For every game I have ever worked on, the community comes up with some pretty weird "theories" and conspiracies about the game, its content, and anything else imagined related to the game. The more complex the game, the more likely a farfetched and insane theory will pop up.

Back in 1998 when the first *Baldur's Gate* game was released, the message boards contained more than a few bizarre theories. *Baldur's Gate* was a role-playing game with a crazy amount of depth and content, and had hundreds of gameplay hours where the player had huge freedom to approach anyway they wanted.

A player on our message boards put forth a rather convoluted series of events a player could do to gain a Vampiric Sword, one that would cause damage and heal the wielder. Sounds bad ass but most definitely did not exist in the game. The poster of this comment swore that it existed and outlined the series of steps it took to attain this "Easter egg[1]"(a hidden feature or joke put into the game by the developers). Reading this post, we were shocked at how huge the thread had become on the message boards of people trying to get the non-existing prize, the speculation on the lore of the weapon, etc. This was the "Elvis sighting" for our game. Some called him a liar while others claimed that they were doing the quest/item combination and were well on the way to getting the Vampiric Sword themselves.

We could not let that stand. In the next update for the game, we added the Vampiric Sword exactly as described by the fan with one minor change—we made the weapon cursed (it healed your target for 1 HP, making it useless for combat). We then added a humorous in-game description, basically saying "This really isn't worth getting, but hey, have fun". Players still found a way to use it by smacking around their own characters with to heal them 1 HP at a time. Players creativity and patience should never be questioned—both are endless.

---

[1] Easter Eggs are hidden features, content or even just jokes the developers put into their games, usually for their own amusement. These can be in the game for years before the public finds them.

Another *Baldur's Gate* in-joke was started by Greg Zeschuk, one of BioWare's founders. Greg liked to make fun of the treasure seeking nature of RPGs in general, and his favourite "loot" to joke was about the Golden Pantaloons. It's fun to say and completely nonsensical in game terms. Many a late night you could hear him shout out "You took the last piece of pizza, but you will never get my Golden Pantaloons!" or some other non-sequitur with that punchline. There was no reason for them to be in-game, but after quoting the joke online a few times and ending up on message boards, we decided to add the item. In fact, the Golden Pantaloons are one of the few items that are part of a quest line that runs through the entire series of four games, rewarding players with the ultimate armour in the game if they follow through and complete it. The whole game series is full of jokes, Easter eggs, and other shenanigans that only a handful of people on the planet know about and/or would find funny. Heck, my evil doppelgänger is even in the game (complete with my severed head as the icon). Lesson here is don't make fun of your designers when they are in the midst of designing a quest.

Interacting with gamers: we are all in this together

Making games is unlike almost any other type of entertainment from the fact a game is interactive when consumed and the amount creators interact with those who use their products is much higher. Message boards, trade shows, Twitch streams[2], YouTube, Twitter, and any other social media has game makers talking directly to fans and detractors alike.

This can be both good and bad depending on who is involved. Internet manners and etiquette have definitely suffered the last decade, but the chance to get direct feedback is very valuable, and everyone is trying to keep these avenues open and productive.

Message boards and talking to the community

Message boards, feedback, and player interaction have become buzzwords synonymous with quality games. Listening to players and their thoughts to steer a game's content, balance, and future are key to making a successful game.

This is mostly true, but the parts less than accurate are also a deadly trap that can sink any title no matter the potential. On a high-

---

[2] Twitch is a streaming service where players can stream video on the internet of them playing a game for anyone to watch. They often commentate and give insights while they play. There is a live chat alongside the video where people watching interact with the streamer.

level user feedback is no different from any other data point, whether it's data gathered from the games performance showing how players are experiencing the game, message boards, focus groups (which are just slightly more organised forms of message boards), or even feedback from the team overall. Each has their place and weight in decision-making, but none should be used exclusively to make any decision.

The best forums and message boards are curated by community managers that not only collate the information and opinions, but also steer the boards and engage them to get the most out of the feedback. Whether it's organisation of the boards themselves, sticky posts at the top of a subheading, to events and theme days that drive specific types of feedback, all this effort helps the information loop between players and developers.

First let's talk about organisation. Each game has its own feature set that message boards should be organised to reflect. Don't go too granular in the breakdown for the subheadings but having everything in a "general" board is equally useless. Threads tend to "explode" and dominate sections for a time, and it's best if a single thread doesn't derail the entire process. It is far better to make certain topics easy for the users to find. If a player wants to find strategies, an FAQ [3], or look for others to play with, these are all very different needs and should be catered to separately.

Next is moderation, making sure that the boards are useful for people. The trend for message boards/forums over the years is heading downwards in quality overall. People seem to think that hyperbole and extremes are the only way to be noticed: "This is the best 'X' ever! And you are an idiot if you think otherwise" or "I can't believe this was made—Hitler was less evil and incompetent". They may be right to go this direction for being noticed (or trolling), but far as usefulness for the actual game and game makers, these comments become pointless "noise". I guarantee that this is NOT the best "X" or worse than Hitler. Now hyperbole is not useful, but it can be civil. Where moderation really comes into play is where civility breaks down—this is rampant. Racist, sexist, and hate-filled threads and comments are not just common but weirdly acceptable in way too many people's minds.

I could write a whole book on the why's and examples, but suffice to say you gain a thick skin pretty darn fast if you choose to frequent even the less shady areas of the internet. Sometimes the

---

[3] FAQ= Frequently Asked Questions

community and other gamers are pretty good at self-policing with an unanswered troll usually posting a few times and leaving if they do not get a bite, but it is far preferable to have a moderator remove them. This isn't for the developer but the innocent bystander who genuinely is looking for info, guidance, or even friends to hang out with and talk about their favourite game.

No game community is full of only idiots and assholes, just as none are toxic free. In general, the more competitive a game is, the more likely bile and vitriol will be spewed forth on even the most benign topics.

Now let's talk about the actual feedback, assuming it is clearly stated, thought out, and not full of hate speech that could be possibly criminal in any other context.

Gamers are gamers. They are not programmers, artists, or designers (for the most part). This means they have no fundamental understanding of the restrictions, technical limitations, or the good sense of a skilled professional in any area of game creation. In general gamers gravitate to the more obvious and "in-your-face" aspect of the perceived issue and posit the most seemingly obvious surface level changes. This is almost never the correct answer— I will explain why.

Games are crazy complex systems with so many factors at play that "just increase the damage of 'X' and it will fix it" is almost always wrong. Now the fact they identified something as not fun is nearly always right. Gamers know what is fun. It is subjective but can never be wrong. If a gamer is not having fun, they are not having fun—there is nothing to argue. What is not subjective is the solutions to actual problems. Say "When I use the shotgun, it feels weak and it's nearly impossible to kill an enemy with it" is totally valid feedback. Posting "Clearly you guys are idiots. Increase the ammo to 10, nerf[4] player health by half, or I am leaving the game" is not. They are saying the exact same issue but only one is useful that the developers can work from, while the other is a designer wannabe acting like a five year old (what we actually think when reading these negative comments) with the goal of posting exclusively to gain a rise out of people.

As of late the online communities, whether message boards, YouTube, or even more mainstream gaming sites, are getting to the level of toxicity that will come to a head at some point. Posting patch notes should not be met with death threats as a response ever—I

---

[4] To "nerf" something is to make it weaker. It refers to the popular toy manufacture known for making toy guns that shoot soft projectiles.

197

mean there is no circumstances in gaming where that behaviour is acceptable. Released in summer 2016, *No Man's Sky* is a perfect example involving the lack of reasonable discourse around a game. Try going to any message board regarding the game. This example is just the latest in a long list of game releases where people's passion outstrips their sense of civility.

In my more frustrated moments, I dream of a two-tiered internet. Tier 1 is is the current situation: an anonymous free-for-all where freedom of speech is paramount. This practice absolutely needs to be protected at all costs. The second is a regulated, curated place where users must use their real name and info. Why? Put your money where your mouth is. If someone is willing to express an opinion, then they should not fear having their real name associated with it. Also;

1) I am tired of trying to get feedback on my own work in a sea of ^%$.

2) I am tired of trying to get info on someone else's work and can't because the first 100 posts are racist/sexist hate.

3) In order to connect with people, we (all of us) should not have to endure this weak-minded attempt of showing force and influence.

My goal is not to silence dissenting views or encourage anything negative, I want to hear about what people don't like about a game as much as I want to hear what they love. Specifically I am talking about the hate and threats based on sex, race, or other harmful speech that most countries have laws against. that the fact I must outline and define civil conversation really angers me.

This awful behaviour is getting to a point where creators will not interface with the public anymore.I used to love visiting message boards and interacting with folks. Lovers and haters alike so long as we can have an actual conversation, I am always game; however, over the last few years this has started to become harder. We don't spend 80 hours a week working on passion projects so we can be threatened and called names. I have it easy—I am white, male, and an English speaker. My colleagues have been in tears because of actual threats over video games.

As creators we choose to interact and take feedback from our players because honestly I think it makes a better game…, we can choose not to as well.

Data, data, data - we need your data (or do we?)

A game I worked on recently called *Block N Load* serves as a good example for several lessons. In this game, players have fantastical heroes with crazy weapons that fight in a *Minecraft*-like world where they can build and destroy anything. Saying this goal was a challenge to keep balanced is a gross understatement. During Beta phase before we launched, one of the characters was called O.P. Juan Shinobi, a ninja. He could jump crazy far and climb walls, and ran around with a katana and shuriken. His job was to move around fast, sneak behind enemy lines, and take down objectives.

Early on we had feedback that OP was weak and had little killing power (this was back at the start of Beta). After watching newer players in action, we discovered that they were missing strikes with the katana—they were not actually making contact when swinging it. After some more feedback and play, we discovered that every melee tool/weapon was ranged at three blocks but Katana was at two. People assumed they should be hitting but were not. They were used to melee ranges of the other tools. It seemed wrong when the character Nigel was swinging his machete at players that could not respond with their primary weapon. We decided that all melee ranges should be normalised, and the Katana was brought up to a range of three. Why did we not reduce the range of the other tools? Build range had been tweaked several times, and we are happy with the feel of the building feature. Making a skybridge or a defensive tower with a lower range by one block would be painful, and we were not going to hurt 50% of gameplay for this one balance change to a hero's ability.

After this change, many players felt that O.P. was just too powerful. We let it play out for a week and collated as much data possible from the kills/deaths/assists for each hero and other sources.

We found that O.P. was at the top of the kills section, but wait, he is also at the top of the character deaths as well. As a concept, O.P. takes high damage but is also a high-risk damage dealer. With him falling into the middle of the K/D/A[1] pack overall, he is close to

---

[1] K/D/A is "Kills", "Deaths", "Assists". In many competitive games, especially first-person shooters, this grouping of statistics are generally used to compare different players level of skill.

his concept. So where does this perception of unbalance come from? Who is experiencing this? Is this even true?

After seeing that O.P. is the most selected hero to play by a high margin, and looking at how many new players are coming into the game every day, we can see that a lot of "noobs"[2] are playing him and most likely poorly.

During this period, we watched a bunch of streams, YouTube videos, and played a ton ourselves for first-hand experience. We found that a good O.P. player was a death machine, and that new players were propping up his death numbers due to their lack of overall skill to even out his K/D/A, but realistically O.P. was a monster for anyone that was half-way competent.

So did the Katana range have anything to do with this? Did we make a mistake? We needed more info. We watched the top O.P. players and what strategies they used to observe their exploits if there were any.

We discovered changing his katana range had very little relation to strategy. The change in attack reach lowered the bar for competent O.P. use so newer players found the character accessible (which was

---

[2] Newbs or noobs are new players to a game, often used as a term of derision by gamers: "Quit being a newb, play better!"

a good change) while experienced players were not any more lethal. What was actually making O.P. crazy powerful was the option to use his shuriken alternate fire (three at once) and swap back to his katana with almost no DPS loss (damage per second): he would start at range, fire. swap, and swing, and if the enemy managed to get out of range for any reason, he could almost instantly swap back to the shuriken and finish them off. This was never intended to be this powerful. Although we wanted some weapon "juggling", there needs to be balance.

For the next update, we did several things to address O.P.'s weapon balance:

1) Ninja Shuriken equip time increased to 0.5 s from 0.25 s.

2) Ninja Shuriken triple throw pre-attack time increased to 0.5 s from 0.3 s, post-attack time reduced to 0.5 s from 0.7 s.

3) Ninja Katana swing time and damage per hit lowered by 25%, sword DPS is same as before. Bleed damage[3] is unchanged.

Now O.P. swung a bit faster (again to help newbs), but his ability to weapon juggle was nerfed so the player must commit more to a fight range. The modifications pushed his stats down for the top

---

[3] Bleed damage is a game term that means the player takes damage over a period of time instead of all at once.

end players to be more in line with the other heroes but as importantly, this did not make it more difficult or less fun for the average or newer player.

My last point is that a game cannot be balanced for everyone all the time. When looking at the more popular games, there is a huge, massive difference in skill between the top players and the average ones. This is regardless of genre or type of game, placing the developer sometimes in a difficult position when balancing gameplay. I touched on it briefly in my example, but the needs and wants between expert and average players are often at odds with each other, so what to do? In general, majority rules—it is foolish to hurt 90% of the community to service 10%. Of course this is very easy to say, but realising that those top 10% usually re the most vocal, on message boards, posting YouTube videos, and streaming on Twitch, pissing them off is the last thing you want to do... so it is quite the tightrope walk at times.

We usually don't get it perfect the first try, but through as many interactions and iterations as the publisher and developer can possibly afford, we get there step-by-step: interacting with our community of players, finding as much data as we can get our hands on, and using our experiences as creators to make the right calls to create the best game possible.

Data is everywhere whether it's typed, posted, snapped as a picture on a phone, consider it public domain. Now this may not be strictly true, but treat your information like that is the case. So what does this have to do with gaming?

When making a game as game makers, we want as much information about players, how they play, what they like, and what they don't like about playing our games. This practice is how we improve games and make them better long-term. Over the last ten years, telemetry[4] about how games are played has been sent directly to us and standard now. We have to ask players if we want any personal data, such as names, emails, or IP addresses (player location), and many accept. The vast majority of players we don't need or want this extra info unless we are trying to sort out something very specific, but I am getting ahead of myself.

So what do we use this data for? No modern game is ever complete—we update, patch, and improve the game long after shipping. Almost all games have a multiplayer element that we want to make sure lasts players for months, if not years of enjoyment, so we keep adding to make the game better.

---

[4] Telemetry is raw data about the game and how it's played which is automatically sent to a secure server.

Let's use a first-person shooter as an example. In a single-player campaign, these are examples of data we would track:

- How long the player took to complete each mission
- Where, when, and how often the player died and the cause
- What weapons and equipment the player is using or not
- Player session length
- Where the player went in each map
- Progression rate if there is XP or levelling, etc.

What do publishers and developers do with all this data? We create huge charts and spreadsheets, and then balance the game to make it more fun. If 20% of our players get stuck on a certain puzzle, let's make a change so it is more obvious. If 60% of the players never use weapon "X", let's look closer and determine why.

A multiplayer game/feature is much the same, but balance is far more important due to ongoing and ever-changing player skills as they improve, tactics changing, and (sadly) bugs being found. An unbalanced multiplayer feature is death to a game—the community has no tolerance for it and shouldn't since they have a huge amount of choice for their gaming time. When a game is unbalanced, skill no longer dictates who wins. What is the point of playing a game like that?

Examples of data we would track in a multiplayer game:

- Seconds to death (length of time from spawning until killed by another player)
- Where players are killed in the map
- Weapon and equipment usage
- Class choices (if the game has them)
- Map choices
- Win/Loss ratio for different aspects and loadouts
- Length of time to get into a match via matchmaking

Plus hundreds and hundreds of other information points to get a better idea on how the game is being played. When creating the game, we have spreadsheets, designs, and an idea in our heads on how something will play and feel. Until players actually play the game, we don't know if whether our assumptions indeed work. This data helps us impartially check to see if features are lining up and where it doesn't. If something seems really weird or case specific, that's the only time game developers may want more personal information about a specific player. The player may be doing something we never considered or have unique setups in hardware, software, or any number of other items where the mass data will not provide insight into the issue. This is where balancing really comes in. So how do we balance the game?

The first stop is the message boards. There is often a lot of hyperbole surrounding any message board, but general sentiment is a good place to start. Often someone posts "'X' character killed me so nerf 'X'" without understanding the reasons or even the bigger picture; rarely taking into account the skill level of all the players involved or are quoting the perfect storm where "X" should be great. This does not mean the feedback is invalid but needs to be vetted very carefully. As a whole, message boards are the best place to discover people's perception of weak/powerful game elements which is worth a lot.

The second stop is game data from play sessions. We track data on every little item in the game. Every death, weapon firing, and tick of damage including where/when it happened. Data does not lie; however, like message boards it does not take into account player skill and specific situations, just cold, hard facts. This data is great to point out problem areas, power spikes, or lulls but provides no real information on the cause. We use data to confirm or disprove message board sentiment. Someone posts "'Y' is very weak in the game", but checking the data reveals "Y" is the top of the Kills/Deaths/Assists table indicating it's not the case. Doesn't change the perception (by definition it cannot be wrong), but we are facing a different problem that will require a different solution in this case.

Last stop is our own experience, both in playing games ourselves and as game makers. This is where we take the raw feedback, match it with data, and then figure out what we need to do about it. We have to take into account the entire game design, the desired gameplay, and rules we have imposed. Balancing a character does not happen in a vacuum, and we have to consider other characters, present and future. In this case, as game makers also have to balance the fun of both playing the character and being their victim too.

Making a splash, getting noticed: Tradeshows and PR

After one of our first big E3s at BioWare, 1999, we spent the last night before heading back having a good time to celebrate the show. We ended up roaming all over LA, hitting bars and checking out the local culture. We were all Canadians, mostly from northern rural areas and this was for many of us the first time to LA or even a large city.

Kalvin Lyle, a childhood friend of mine and artist at BioWare, and many others were partners in crime that evening, and to be honest, it was all a blur after 8 p.m. We were in Hollywood—I remember that. Hustler Hollywood was an adult store I vaguely recall entering then off to... another bar? I don't know. We somehow managed getting back to our hotel in Santa Monica, and I remember being jarred conscious by the wake-up call from the front desk. We had a pretty early flight and had all lost track of each other at some point. It was a real train wreck and I was worried that many would miss the flight home. We met down in the lobby to catch a taxi to LAX, and boy were we in a sorry state. Half were still drunk in various states of dishevelled. We got to the airport and were standing in line to get through security, trying to piece together what actually happened the night before. "We went to the rainbow room? Ok, didn't recall that. The standard hotel—ya, I remember being there. They had these women in empty fish tanks doing homework... weird." The line through to security was long but moving. We were about ten people from the front when I pitched into the conversation remembering that we went to Hustler of Hollywood. A round of smiles and laughing as each remembered their experience of that store... all except for Kalvin. He just kind of blanched a bit. Hard to see as he was sort of green from feeling rather hungover, but I caught it. "Hey, what's up?" I asked. He said, "I now remember being at that store. I remember buying something... studded leather underwear." I laughed. Not so crazy considering what he could have bought there. The line shuffled forward, we were nearly at the security check. "That's not the problem... The problem is, I think I am wearing them right now," he said just as we were next to the metal detector. I have never laughed so hard and considering our hangovers, we were lucky that none of us threw up on the spot. Kalvin ran off to the bathroom, checking/changing his undergarment, and hurriedly got back in line. We barely made it to our gate in time, but it all worked out. There's a lesson here boys and girls—keeping track of what you buy when travelling abroad is not just important for customs.

That was not the end of our trip either. We were all excruciatingly hungover, and flying in that state is about the least amount of fun you can experience. It is a four hour or so flight from LA to Edmonton and every minute was pain. We were roughly an hour out of Edmonton when the announcement came on. "Uhh, this is your pilot speaking. We, uhhh, are getting reports of some pretty serious thunderstorms in the vicinity and, uhh, will be trying to fly around what we can, but there will be some pretty serious turbulence." Seatbelt lights came on and the real fun began. I have flown hundreds, no thousands of times in my life, and this was some of the worst turbulence I have ever experienced. When the crew straps everything down followed by putting all four points of their seatbelt on, you know it's going to be a rough ride.

So here we are, nearly vomiting before the plane started to bounce around, gaining and losing hundreds of feet randomly every few seconds while trying to keep it together. The "sideways" buffets were the worst. We were at the back of the plane and I swear seeing the plane flexing as we were bashed around. The pilot came on again. "Uhh, as you can tell we are in some rather rough weather up here, and we won't be able to really avoid much of it from hear on in." *What, we were avoiding some of it? Lies!* I thought while surveying the BioWare crew in all their shades of grey and green, many using sick bags. He continued. "So, uhh, we are going to try landing in Edmonton as fast as possible as they are shutting down the airport due to the weather, and we don't have a clear path to redirect to Calgary." *Fantastic.*

The descent was the most insane I have ever experienced. I swear, the pilot basically just pointed the nose down and "went for it" while as if Godzilla himself was beating on the plane like it owed him money. The final and only approach was extremely violent until the last 15 feet where it just calmed to nothing, ending in a smooth touchdown. Once all the wheels were down we were buffeted violently again, nearly pushing us off the runway; however, we safely taxied to the gate and all clapped. I have never understood why people clapped on landing when the crew did their job, but that is until now. Those men and women were gods, conquering nature all with a calm "Take uhh... that!". As we were deplaning, the airport was literally turning off runway lights and shutting down as tornados were touching down over the area. Ya, a fun and memorable E3 that year.

A great game needs great marketing

Making a great game is pointless if no one knows about it. Getting a game in front of players can be a difficult. There is a limited amount of time and space that journalists, fans, and partners can spend promoting. Even if a title can get into the fray, there are so many games, gadgets, and general noise that fill our streams and social media that standing out has become a bigger problem than getting the actual coverage. Add in the one last complication that the "big boys" like Activision and Electronic Arts are willing to spend hundreds of millions of dollars marketing their key games, and smaller developers can find themselves choked out of the mainstream venues very quickly. Platforms such as Steam has dozens of well designed, fun games that PC players never heard about and let alone played due to this saturation and competition.

So how do companies promote their games?

Magazines (both online and print)

Activision in the early to mid-2000s was very good at treating us well, especially if we had to go the extra mile they would too. When I first moved to Los Angeles from Canada, my girlfriend and soon to be wife stayed behind for the first year. Every month she would fly down from Vancouver or I would go north to visit her.

In January, the *Quake 4* press tour was making the rounds. Other than some advisory/feedback stuff, I was not involved with *Quake 4*, but the game was being made by Activision's shooter group which included comrades-in-arms and good friends. There was a press tour stop in New York where the "general" press would get a preview the game. General press is defined as non-gamer publications, *WIRED*, national newspapers, etc. that have some gaming coverage but were not games focused. The Producer of the game could not make it due to an emergency (I forget exactly what it was), but Activision was desperate to get someone familiar with the title, could talk to the press competently, and would be able to get folks excited about the game.

I was pulled aside by Activision's Executive Producer for the project asked if I would go to New York for a couple days and represent the game. I was about to get on a plane back to Canada because January 21st is my wedding anniversary, and I had not seen my wife in over a month. They would not have asked but were in a tight spot. The press tour could not be cancelled or rescheduled, and because *Quake* was an id Software title, Activision did not have a long list of people that could fill in. id software were rock stars in the industry and rather particular on whom they worked with or allowed to represent them. I was on this list. I explained that it was just not possible if I wanted to remain married. They countered: "What if we flew your wife to New York and extend your stay a few days and covered all the costs? You could have your anniversary in New York, nice hotel and all free if you spend the first few days helping us out during the day." This magazine press tour was that important to them. I called my wife and asked what she thought. Neither myself nor my wife had been to New York, and that deal was pretty sweet. It was a compromise—honestly, I think I got the better end of that particular deal. The role publications play in getting the word out about a game is crucial to being found by players.

When I first started making games, in a print magazine like *PC Gamer* a cover story or review could make or break a title. Nowadays, however, print magazines are falling by the wayside, especially in tech and game industries. They have long lead times (two to three months) with circulations dwindling greatly over the last ten years. Publishers still like using them as they tend to be more "trusted" sources since they are not some person on a message board posting an opinion but tend to be writers, gamers, and journalists. It is a great shame that the move away from print has been so thorough.

All is not lost. Many of these journalists have moved to their online counterparts, and the quality of these publications has risen greatly over the years. There are still contentious articles and other shenanigans, but the same complaints have been levelled at print magazines in the beginning, leaving online publications in good company. Online sources have the advantage of being instantly relevant in seconds with edits and updates made in real-time. There has been a huge increase in the number of writers and sources which enabled sites to specialise. Many niche games can get coverage, where before they were limited to a few dozen print magazines and would most likely never be mentioned.

Social Media

Twitter and Facebook have become so ubiquitous in business, and games are no exception. From "Likes", posts, to contests and other promotions, the vast majority of game promotion starts on social media sites. If you are looking for a free code, the latest screenshots, or interviews, the best bet is to check these sources first.

The messages themselves are usually not a big deal, they tend to push the reader to the actual content location. Having marketing or community people dedicated to ensuring that the accounts are useful and active helps, especially targeting by using bite-sized updates that draw in people to click the links for more detail.

YouTube

It's not just cat videos and Russian traffic accidents (seriously, after watching dozens if crash videos, can anyone drive there?). Official videos for the game in development always hit YouTube, generally arriving on that site first. Gone are the days of hosting anything locally—let the owners of YouTube, Google, do it. Not only is the hosting free, but the bandwidth is essentially unlimited.

YouTube has become a critical part of gam marketing that now we have schedules built in and specifically made tools for making videos of games much easier. The extra amount of awareness generated by having regular videos being posted is amazing: developer diaries, highlighting specific elements of the game in short informative videos, to anything that builds interest from the fan base. Setting aside the time to make these videos will help get coverage and folks noticing the game.

This venue for information has gotten so large and powerful that they have basically replaced traditional print magazines for their impact on gamers' purchasing habits. If someone like *jacksepticeye* or *PewDiePie* likes or dislikes a game, millions of gamers will know and be influenced by their reviews.

Twitch and other streaming services

One of the newer additions to the pantheon of promotion is Twitch, a streaming website where people can play games and stream live to anyone who cares to watch. Streams have anywhere from zero to a hundred thousands of viewers, and there are real internet celebrities being made in this new venue. What's different is that the publishers or game maker are not driving this promotion. Publishers and developers do have official channels on Twitch, but it's the fans who really take up the mantle and do all the work with their own take/spin on broadcasting. Fans will play a decent game for endless hours, basically making an endless commercial if they are enjoying it with thousands of people watching.

There are sponsored streams where the publisher or dev pay people to stream (same with YouTube videos), but the majority of the streams are not sponsored with the hosts playing because they genuinely enjoy the game. This is my favourite avenues for promotion since it's honest. There are no scripts, no checklist of features to be rattled off, just a gamer and a game playing for other gamers. Next to the stream is a chat where the viewers get to interact with the streamer, asking questions, telling jokes, and generally hanging out. It's very social and more like going to a friend's house to check out a game... except thousands are there and some folks may even know what they are talking about. There are downsides , but this venue seems to be heading in a good direction with a very level playing field. Anyone can stream, anyone can watch.

Block N Load streams were posted sporadically with viewers going from a hundred to a few thousand. Often there would only be a handful of streams with just their friends watching. Then there was this Russian channel— 500k of viewers consistently, and he played our game for weeks. I have no idea who this gamer was, how he heard about us, or even what he was saying about our game. He clearly had a loyal and large following, and seemed to like our game. It's one of those weird stories you hear about some unknown artist who "is really big in Japan". Apparently, we had quite the Russian following since this gamer was quite the influencer. He was really good too—played all the different heroes, knew some great strategies, and was enthusiastic when playing. We could not ask for anything more and could not have made or done a better job promoting our game than he could. Twitch is a great equaliser, the best access to a level playing field currently.

Trade shows

The biggest trade show is still E3, the Electronic Entertainment Expo. Having been located at several venues, is the event usually takes place in Los Angeles around June every year. E3 is the biggest, loudest, and craziest games convention in the world. No one ever forgets the first time going. The first few days are industry people only, but the expo usually opens up to anyone over the age of 18. The games shown by the different makers will not be found on the shelf but will be for sale in the coming year or so. This means participants see and even play games that are unavailable to the public for months. As a gamer, this is amazing. As a games maker, this is pure hell.

Imagine working insanely hard to make a great game but are months (or more) away from shipping it. The Publisher says "Ok, E3 is a few months away. What are we going to show?" *Show? ...SHOW!? The game isn't done, it barely runs at all, and most of it doesn't even exist yet.* While considering what can be built to run for that time and remembering full well it will not have been optimised or even through a decent QA pass most likely, you have the sober realization that people will be judging this as the final quality of the game no matter how many disclaimers are placed all over the loading screen.

Don't forget we need a trailer movie to put in the company demo reel (remember there are no final assets yet!) and oh, some screenshots for the press kit. Oh, plus can we have like five or ten of your guys go to the show and run the game at the booth? We know they are crazy busy trying to make the game, but to show it off the best, we really should have the folks who know the most about it on hand. Make sure it's perfect too, please, as every journalist ever will be there poking holes in whatever we show and comparing the game to every other one at the tradeshow, even ones that may be nearly done or spent ten times more than us on making it. No pressure.

These demands end up being a huge distraction, pushing the dev to focus on tasks out of order that would logically be followed when making the game. The stress levels are high at E3 to have a great demo, win awards, etc., which can make or break the successful launch of a game. This "broadside" only happens once. After the first E3, developers learn to plan for it ahead of time, making allowances in the schedule and ensuring specific features are ready for the Expo, plus other marketing requirements. But that first one... man..it hurts.

Then there is the show itself. You arrive a few days early to set up, which depends greatly on who the publisher is and how intricate the booth is. Ever seen a tank being driven through a back entrance of a convention centre while dodging spaghetti-strung network cables and go-go dancer cages? Visit an E3 set-up. If the game is online, requiring network connections, etc., be prepared for some insanity. Everyone else does. We are talking thousands... and thousands of people with their IT, inundating the convention centre's

IT with questions, and trying to get everything sorted from network, power, to borrowing cranes and other bits needed for the set-up of these multimillion dollar booths. It's insane.

The booths are over the top. Huge sound systems blasting music, full light shows only found at a stadium concert set-up, and anything else they can think of to grab attention even if the idea is remotely linked to the titles showing. Costumed characters, vehicles, and celebrities are standard. They also tend to give away t-shirts, posters, and other tchotchkes with logos, characters, and brightly coloured bits that entice people to pop in and take a look at their games. The booths themselves ebb and flow far as "crazy" goes. Some years it was full of literal go-go dancers in cages at the Konami booths (with a k, and an o, and a n-a-m-i song will forever be burned into my head) to more recent years where presentations were slightly more business-like.

The days at the show were not much better. You get there early, do a final testing of the setup. A video card is bound to die, the network will fail, a server will overheat, SOMETHING will go wrong. Don't forget the game code running has not been thoroughly tested or optimised so literally every single time anyone goes up to a machine you hold your breath, waiting.... wincing when you see them do something a little bit "off the expected path" on your "bubble gum and tinfoil held together" demo.

So, who are the people playing? For the most part E3 is for two very different groups of people. The first are journalists getting a sneak peek of what is coming up from all the big franchises. Usually gamers themselves for the most part, it is generally easy demoing for them. They get it, act like professional, and have most likely been to E3 before. They generally understand that the game is not done and may crash, and they don't have to include that in the preview or E3 coverage. They tend to ask good questions, are enthusiastic, and always push for that inside bit of information about a feature or detail that will make their article stand out.

The second group of folks are the buyers. These are generally not gamers but work for big distributers like Walmart, deciding what and how much to buy of any particular game to stock their shelves. They were probably at a convention for crockery last week, and next week it's clothing. Some of them are gamers, or at least they specialise in tech or something related, but not always. You tend to focus on the big bullet points when talking to them, and trying to convince them how well it will sell versus is the quality of the game. They tend to not have game specific questions but more about when it ships, what marketing is being spent, etc.

The end result is being on your feet for 12 hours a day for four or five days and rather stressed; however, there are some nice upsides. First and obviously is exposure for the game. There is no higher concentration of press in one place on the planet for games. By having a good show and winning awards, the hype of the game increases measurably. Second, this is an industry event, meaning that the whole show is full of people who make games for a living. Visit with old friends and co-workers, meet new people who share similar likes and experiences... and go drinking. Yes, there are a lot of parties after each day of the show thrown by different companies and exhibitors, and generally have some good food and free booze. Invites are required to many of these functions, but many are given out rather freely. After a long stressful day, exhibitors stay out to the wee hours of the morning cavorting with some cool people. Of course, the exhibitors get up early the next day to repeat the whole cycle. There have been many a booth operator looking a little green under the gills struggling to survive the day.

Times are changing: The death of the mid-range game

Crysis was a first-person shooter made by Crytek and published by Electronic Arts. Released in 2007 to great acclaim, the technology pushed the boundaries of what a game could look like, and was and still is a benchmark for graphical fidelity. The sequel was greenlit and released in 2011. Again the game was well-received with the addition of a more solid multiplayer mode (which I was lucky enough to be a part of the team), and the game hit the gamer mainstream. After rave reviews and millions in sales, a third game was created. We shipped the third instalment in 2013, continuing the success of the franchise with the same rave reviews while continual progressing in both gameplay and visuals. It has been a few years since then, so where is the next *Crysis* game? In an industry with endless sequels from games (*Call of Duty* is up to 12 or something), it is 2017, where is *Crysis 4*?

I was part of the pitch for *Crysis 4*, working with others on the features that the game would have, how to push gameplay, and what we thought was next not only for that game but on becoming industry leaders in the genre. The plan was ambitious yet approachable. Everyone seemed happy with the direction, and we waited for the "go ahead" to start production, but it never came. There was one thing that I did not count on when considering the franchise future, and I only came to realise after the fact that there was a shift in the games industry's attitude towards "mid-tier games". One of the major factors was there was no place anymore for games like *Crysis* at big publishers like Activision and Electronic Arts.

The *Crysis* franchise, although popular, was never going to unseat games like *Call of Duty* or EA's own *Battlefield* series of games in terms of sales or prominence. This goal was never the intention, we wanted to be the best of the second-tier games. AAA in quality, but not quite in scope and certainly not in marketing. The problem is the costs of making a game like *Crysis* are very nearly the same as going all out on one of those top-tier games. This made the executives at publishers ask the question "Why take the risk when we can just focus on our own AAA titles?"

The landscape of making games has drastically changed over the last few years because of development costs. Where once there was a wide spectrum of studios making games of all descriptions, the industry is now in a state where the "second-tier" of games and game makers have all but disappeared. Why this has happened and where these game makers have gone is an interesting story, and the transition has been anything but subtle.

The rise of development costs

With each successive platform generation, the costs of making the actual games increase significantly. In the 1990s with the PS1 and Xbox, a few million dollars was needed to create AAA quality titles, but by the time of PS3 and Xbox 360 the costs were 10 to 15 million dollars to make the equivocal games. At the end of this present generation, games are 20 to 50 million dollars to make, and as we transition into Xbox One and PS4 budgets, 50 million dollars will be the standard for top-tier games. Why has this increased so much?

Scope

A player model used to be a few hundred polygons and textures measuring in at kilobytes of memory. Now it is millions of polygons which are then textured with an asset that would consume more memory than an entire game back a generation ago. With very clever programming, these detailed assets work in real-time environments which previously existed only in cutscenes. Add in multiplayer, co-op, and social gaming elements, now the challenges, persistence, and scope of game are unrecognisable to when I started 20+ years ago. A big game on the newest console or PC from the 1990s or even 2000s easily will run on the phone in the pocket of the average consumer right now. Things definitely have changed.

Fidelity

This added fidelity has drastically changed the amount of work required to get assets into the game. Creating a standard character in the required about 1 artist working in 2D, creating something 128 x 128 pixels which would take a day or two at most. This artist was also quite likely the person who would be animating the character and doing anything else related to the sprite (name of a 2D bitmap). Today it takes a modeller several weeks to make a single 3D character model that contains millions of times more info/detail than any sprite. Odds are the artist is not the one texturing the character (giving it skin/colour), and further someone else will be rigging and animating it. Each one of those steps have been split up and given to people with specialised skills, and every one of those processes taking days or weeks. A character went from taking a few days to taking many weeks or even months from idea to in-game. The art team must be much bigger to produce this level of detail and create a larger number of characters compared to years ago. Art teams are nearly always the largest component of any development team for this reason.

Multiplayer

Multiplayer as a feature is common, practically required for any game nowadays. Not only was this not the case in the past, but even when it was the feature set and breadth of the mulitplayer mode, the then and now are so different and cannot be compared. A game now must have dozens if not hundreds of servers spread around the world providing best performance for players. The sheer number of players online on a single popular game in 2016 would dwarf the numbers of all online players in 1996. The game needs the architecture and servers to support multiplayer, and contingencies when things go wrong, hackers attempt DDoS [1] attacks, and any other unforeseen circumstance.

---

[1] DDoS is a type of Denial of Service attack where multiple machines flood a target system (or server) with messages and requests to slowing the server down or even "crash" it. They are often global and distributed by bot nets which can make it very hard to defend against.

The multiplayer game feature itself is far more than allowing gamers to see each other while playing. Players must be able to group up, share experiences, and compare progress and performance against those of their friends and strangers alike. They want to customise their game play, see progress in their characters, and feel like their skill determines the match/game's outcome while the game plays lag[2]-free, never lose connections, and smooth and flawlessly.

This leads into persistence[3]. Role-playing games were far more popular in the past and have for the most part died out (with obvious exceptions, but as a rule it stands). I argue that this is not entirely the case—what happened is that RPGs have been integrated into other genres of games. You cannot play a first-person shooter now without unlocks, character progression, and straight-up experience points earned while playing. It is a RPG. Same could be said about every other genre. I think it's a great addition to give players a sense of accomplishment, progression, goals, and social outlet if done right. It also means that even a "simple" game genre is no longer simple.

---

[2] Lag is when there is latency, usually manifesting pauses between when you do something in the game and the server registering it as "complete".

[3] Persistence is when something is done in game, shown to everyone participating, and stays as a permanent part of the gaming experience for everyone. The next time you log on that change or progress still exists.

These systems take a lot of design, programming, UI, and balancing work in addition to the backbone of the game genres. Mix in that the game should be all persistent, shared online, and used to challenge not only one player but all other players too, becoming a very complex and intertwined set of features that expanded what is required in order to make a good game. All of this takes time to make and balance... including lots and lots of time and money.

Team size

To make games with that fidelity the team sizes have grown incredibly. Teams were 15 to 25 people in the mid-1990s, delivering the content and quality at the highest level. As the technology and requirements increased, people specialised. Studios would not just have "programmers" but a graphics programmer, network programmer, gameplay specialist, and A.I. expert. Artists became 3D character modellers, weapon modellers, environment texture artists, user interface designers, animators, riggers, and a whole host of compartmentalised specialties required to make a game. There is a reason that the credits screens at the end of a game run for 10+ minutes. Teams were now several hundred people directly making content for the game, plus many more in management and support to keep these people focused and producing the game efficiently.

The rise of the game franchise

In the mid-1990s, if a game sold one million units worldwide it was considered a massive hit. It only cost a few million dollars to make a AAA top-rated, top selling game. Often these games were made for far less. Since that quainter time, one game more than any other has ruined PC/console gaming, and I was a small part of it. *Call of Duty*, originally developed by Infinity Ward and published by Activision, may have not been the first big franchise but is certainly used as the poster child in the gaming community of what happens when franchises get big and continue to create sequels ad infinitum.

So, what did the *Call of Duty* franchise do? Although not the only franchise, they were one of the first to really capitalise on their success. By capitalise I mean market the hell out of it. Back in the beginning of the franchise, a marketing budget for a 10 million dollar AAA game in the early 2000s was maybe half, so add another 5 million or so at the time. *Call of Duty* took several sequels to really hit their stride, but marketing jumped firmly on board unlike anyone else I had ever seen at that point. The latest marketing budget for a *CoD* game was rumoured to be over 100 million dollars. So how does that "ruin" anything?

I had mentioned previously that publishers are all about limiting risk, and this new element changed the meaning. With escalating costs of development and enormous spending in marketing, a single title becomes higher risk to the point that any element of additional risk is basically unacceptable. "Sure bets" makes these publicly traded company stockholders happy. Fewer new intellectual properties were being made, and fewer titles in general were started within the big publishers who now focused on the games that made the most money. On the surface this makes complete sense, and in the short-term is understandable. The long-term changes resulting from this focus were far reaching and are still being felt today.

Sequels are conservative by nature and slow to progress in the evolution of gameplay. These sequels are the direct result of publishers playing it "safe" with their huge investments. New IP[4] is few and far between, and treated often as a red-headed step child with far less focus, effort, and spending from a publisher until the game can prove itself with sales, which creates a self-fulfilling prophesy of failure. If a publisher cannot afford to spend $50+ million on development and $100 million on marketing, they are not

---

[4] IP stands for intellectual property.

making an AAA game right now. The game will not get ad space, shelf space, and marketing share of the heavy hitters, putting the title at a distinct disadvantage.

Worse yet for us all, including publishers, is that franchises wane, Without new IP in the pipeline, when a franchise does finally die out, the publisher is left flat-footed as a business, and the gamers are left with only disappointing sequels to play. The *Tony Hawk Pro Skater* skateboarding franchise saved Activision in the late 1990s as a company. No lie, the publisher would have gone bankrupt without this series and were teetering on the brink at the time. The first *Tony Hawk* game came out, doing fairly well and received great reception. The sequels were marketed far better once they understood the game, earning significant profit. The franchise ran for a decade with 14 titles, making huge sums of money but died as other franchises took over. *Guitar Hero*, another huge money maker for Activision, was a major part of their business plan for many years, but the franchise is now dead. *Call of Duty* will get there too—when is anyone's guess, but all empires fall. This time is different since there is very little in the pipeline that could replace *CoD* within Activision's current or upcoming roster. Without investment in new teams and IP, there is little chance for something new to come along.

Publishers focusing on safer bets

With these increased costs, it is surprising very few have been pushed downstream to consumers. Game titles cost ten times the amount compared to a decade ago while the actual cost at the shop has moved very little, so the only way games are profitable is to sell more. Many more units are required to break-even, let alone make profit. This means games must be available on more platforms, more approachable (hard core gamers call it dumbed down), and marketed far harder to increase the numbers of players buying the game. With the risk increasing, publishers could no longer afford the "shotgun" method of creating games: funding four or five titles and one paying off would more than cover the costs of the rest. Focusing on the sure bets leads to *Call of Duty 9*, *Battlefield 6*, and *Football Manager 10* while critically acclaimed but lesser selling games don't get sequels or funded in the first place. Again, this short-term practice makes perfect sense, but 18 months in the future if the pipe is empty, there will be nothing to fill gaps or shortfalls should any of the pillars fail.

Ebb and flow of headcount

This is becoming far more common and found in other industries such as TV and film. These industries have a small production team at its core, contracting the people required to create the production and hiring the actors to deliver performances. Film, edit, and add effects/post production then release the product with everyone involved going their separate ways. If starting another project, re-contracting starts from scratch even though people who work well together often get rehired, but often there is no guarantee. The advantages are clear, having only the people needed at the right time. Everyone is on contract and understands it is "just for this thing". Doing a good job on set means most likely being hired again, but at the end of this fixed term contract you are done.

The games industry is starting to look this way. The team starts small, a nucleus beginning on the initial design and prototype. Once this first phase completes, the team is ramped up by adding dozens of people, artists, programmers, designers, and management as support, and once the game is completed everyone but the core team is let go. The difference for the games industries is that people are not on short-term contracts, no one tells them up front that it is a short-term gig, and it always seems to hit as a surprise. In the past, after the game ships companies have a huge oversupply of extra artists and programmers who can't really do much because unless the developer is structured exceedingly well and hasmultiple projects going on simultaneously, these game makers cannot start the new project until the "nucleus" has complete the foundations.

We need the other shoe to drop and actually adopt the whole system, not just the convenient part for publishers. If everyone goes to contract, there are huge impacts to budgets and other elements of the game making process. Will you move to another city or country for a year's worth of work only to find yourself unemployed in a foreign land? This works for Hollywood because everyone lives in LA. Developers pay more for some positions due to their transitory nature. A top programmer that is not necessarily "nucleus" can command an awful lot moving to Poland for a few months of work with someone paying that cost. Centres of development such as Montreal, andLos Angeles have an advantage with the critical mass of projects starting and finishing all the time. While other places such as Edmonton (home of BioWare) or Nottingham (home of Crytek UK), options are severely limited once a stint of work is completed.

Right now it is getting even scarier as AAA development teams have hundreds of members. When a team or developer ships a game, everyone holds their breath wondering if they have a job next month. Add in when one of these mega teams gets scaled down, hundreds of people flood the job market at once, forcing many to pack up families and move, often immigrating to another country or location.

I have never seen an industry where the workforce moves often as the games industry.

Other influences: Used games

The reason why companies such as EA had an "online pass" program for playing second hand games online was not to gouge players but help cover the overall costs of creation and long-term support. But why were game creators losing money? Stores such as GAME in the UK were selling used copies of games to players in huge numbers. Being able to buy older games second hand is good not only for gamers on a budget, but this market enables a second life for older great games that should be played by many people as possible.

When a game is sold by a retailer as second hand, not a penny goes to the actual game makers while 100% of the profit goes to the retailer. Face value this is not a big deal for older games. The problem was that retailers were selling brand new trade-in games while new releases of the very same title were on the shelf. Worse yet, the retailer would promote the used versions over the new. Take a new game to the counter to buy, and the retail worker would ask, "We have a used version of this, saves you $4. Would you like that?" Of course anyone would. Plus that $44 game is pure profit to the retailer. Meanwhile the game makers get nothing. Gamers got wise to this and would buy a new game then trade-in during the first few weeks after they played for store credit, followed by buying the next used "new" game. This practice was is so prevalent and successful the majority of profits for GameStop, GAME and other second hand retailers were made from used sales, not new. Trading in games is not going away any time soon and the industry just has to deal with it.

One of the ways this has become less of an issue is that many games have an online component that is compelling to players and tied to their gamer account. Although single player games can easily be bought and sold used, the multiplayer element is "consumed" when played online for the first time and attached to a player's personal online account. If the multiplayer component is fun, compelling, and helps players enjoy the game for months on end, this sales practice becomes a good solution.

Mobile gaming

The rise of mobile gaming has impacted AAA PC and console gaming. Since 2008, big publishers have been looking for ways to join this new platform. Whether growing internal teams or outright buying existent successful developers, these companies have been dumping incredible amounts of resources and effort into this new endeavour. Publishers have a finite amount of money and ability to focus, and the attention poured into mobile gaming came mainly at the expense of the mid-range games. Why spend 20 million dollars on a mid-tier game when spending one million dollars on a mobile game that if it succeeds can make the same amount of profit? In fact publishers can fail 20 times on making a mobile title before spending the same amount: 1/20th the risk for the same profit is a no brainer for money people who are responsible to shareholders. So the big AAA games with huge followings get to stay for profit and bragging rights reasons, but anything else is up for debate while the middle ground on PC and consoles have suffered.

Free to Play games: A new(er) way to make money

I loathe spending money when I don't have to. I am the anti-poster child for any payment method that is micro transaction based. So why then does my credit card have a long list of trading card purchases for Blizzard's *Hearthstone* game? This game has been made popular on many platforms including iOS, so I broke down and decided to play on my iPad but was determined there was no way I'd spend actual money. After building a basic deck (it is a combat/trading card game), going through the tutorials, and thoroughly enjoying myself, I wanted to build a proper warlock deck but was short on a few key cards. Telling myself that I can wait and just play with the cards received from normal playing lasted about three hours tops... and then I caved and purchased a few packs. Frustrated that I broke down and spent money, I decided to take a break and play another game, *Clash Royale*.

A deceptively simple game, build an army via cards (*what is with all these great collectible type card games?*) and have short but fun battles to earn currency, chests, and chances for new and better hero cards. The designers implemented a brilliant, and I mean genius, way to reward players for their time with chests on timers. The option to spend real money speeds up opening, but players are not limited by "energy" like other Free to Play games which is a mechanic I despise. *That's ok, I can just wait for the chests to open.* Again, a few hours later I was on a roll and a promotion within my grasp but needed a few good upgrades to push through... *Ahh crap, I spent money.* I seemed to be wandering from minefield to minefield, and my non-spending stance was failing rather hard.

Fine, time to leave mobile gaming. This is ridiculous and surely just a sign of the platform's state. Time to switch and fire up the PC for some "real" games. League of Legends is a fantastic game— I have dumped hundreds of gaming hours into it and really like playing bottom lane with a character called Thresh. I have gotten fairly decent with him even when playing with random teams, but how do I show off that I care about and am good at this character? *I know! I will buy a skin so others can... crap, just did it again.*

At that point I sat down and discovered that I don't mind micro transactions if I feel they are on my terms and worth it. But what does worth it mean to me... or to you?

There are two types of approaches in the industry today: making games that make money or making money by making games. The latter is a sure-fire way to make poor products and are the main reason why "gamers" tend to look at the monetisation of Free to Play, or F2P as it's often shortened, as a negative term.

There are many different ways Free to Play can actually be implemented, but all have the same core of getting a large portion of the game for free to experience. More than a demo, playing is not limited to the first part of the game. This concept is a deeper delivery than a shareware or limited time demo in that the spectrum of features and content played does not degrade or reduce over time; however, it is not a "free" game. There are four main ways that games try convincing players to spend money, and often they use a combination of these different methods with varying levels of success depending on the type of game:

1) Pay to customise

There are a wide range of products that are free for the entire game; however, to stand out games must be unique and allow customising the visuals to enhance the personal aspect of the experience. These customisations can be the player's avatar [1], embodied in a hero/character, a town or other environment a gamer creates, or even badges, colours, and UI elements. For best impact these elements are must be shared outwardly to the community to "show off" choices and preferences.

2) Pay for convenience

This is the most common of Free to Play implementation early on, especially in mobile applications. There are artificial barriers, usually time or energy used to take a "turn" that are put into place that slows the player's progress. For a micropayment a player can temporarily reduce or remove the restrictions, getting extra "turns" if that is the particular restriction preventing play for example. Another common implementation is that building or harvesting a resource will take minutes, hours, or even days. With a small payment, players can have it completed immediately. Technically a player can progress through the entire game, all of it's content without paying anything except this would take an unfeasible amount of time. The line between pay for convenience and pay to

---

[1] The personal representation of "you" in the game.

win can be a bit blurry for some games, but if the content is not hidden behind a money paywall, then the game is not pay to win.

3) Pay for content

Also known as a "paywall", pay for content is one of the oldest methods for micro payments and has its roots back at the dawn of software. Shareware, demos, and other schemes that get people to try out before buying the full product is waning as a Free to Play method overall. The "core" product is offered for free while extra modules and features exist beyond the paywall to enhance the experience. You can still see this method in different incarnations even now. Many Massively Multiplayer Online Games (MMOG) still use a monthly subscription in order for players to gain access, although many are going towards Free to Play with varying degrees of success. Paywalls in general are less popular and fading out as a payment method for game makers.

4) Pay to win

Players can spend real money to buy "power" in the game, providing advantages over anyone who does not spend money. This allows players who spend a lot of money (often called Whales) to dominate play. Without monetising in a big way, players cannot ever consider being in the top measurement of progress or skill in a game. This is the version of F2P that western gamers use as the bogeyman and hold up as the ultimate betrayal of what it is to be a gamer—players don't need skill to "win", just deep pockets. Even a rumour that a particular feature within a game looks like it could be considered P2W[2] and can kill the game with a full on revolt from their gaming community.

This is not a universal viewpoint. In places such as Korea, China, and Russia, P2W is a standard model for many games, and have enormous player numbers and prove to be very successful. Even some players in the west prefer this type of payment model. Players have full-time jobs and other time commitments, and not a lot of time to game. They cannot keep up with those who play eight hours a day and being able to buy items or features that allow them to "keep up" can be very desirable. Fundamentally it's a different way to look at gaming as pure entertainment to be enjoyed rather than as "skill" based activity with the main goal to "win" and be the best.

So which is best method?

---

[2] P2W means Pay to Win.

A game creator should match the system for the type of game—there is no "one" best way to implement. Design the game with the payment systems considered up front. This cannot be retrofitted cleanly or changed mid-stream without serious consequences and development time lost. Some game types lend themselves very well to F2P and competitive play while others do not, and keeping in mind who the gamers are and what their market expects is important as the core design. I personally prefer pay for convenience or customisation as a gamer, but I completely understand why other methods are chosen.

There is also a new trend of games starting out as premium: players pay one price to buy the game and access all its content, and once the demand starts dwindling or the player base falls to a certain level, it goes Free to Play. This form of "double dipping" can work well depending on the time scale. If a game ships and does well but a year later there are not enough players to make it a good experience for everyone, going free to play gives the game a breath of life and brings new people into the community. You may think those who paid full price for a game that is now essentially free would be upset. Many of the original players who payed full price have left already (hence the need to change revenue methods), and those who stayed usually get grandfathered in all sorts of content and perks. Most of the old school players from the original community like the change to F2P because it means new gamers to play against in a waning community, and the alternative is that the game they like dies. Going F2P from premium may not a good plan is when the interval between full price and transitioning to F2P is too short. If after a few months a game switches over, this act can be seen as a cash grab, and only excused assuming the game was in dire straits community-wise and the player base knew it.

Mobile gaming and the Steam Store have seriously impacted what players are willing to pay for games. With the death of the middle-tier games in general, there is a race to the bottom in pricing to get players to play any game, and nothing is lower than free. A minimum amount of players is needed to make a game "work"; this is especially true for multiplayer gaming. Matchmaking, multiple game modes, and proper ranking all require hundreds, if not thousands of players playing simultaneously at all times in every region for these features to behave properly and deliver a good experience. Free to Play is an exceedingly good way to remove all friction between someone seeing a screenshot, video, stream, and message board post before hopping into the game and playing. By having Free to Play, companies are making everyone else's experience, paying people included, better. Free to Play is not going away any time soon and is the go-to method generating revenue for games not on the AAA level of scope.

Other monetising methods

Making games has gotten so expensive that several hundred millions of dollars is required to make a AAA game that publishers and game makers are exploring different ways of creating revenue beyond the launch and initial "boxed" copy picked up at the local gaming store. This money is used to create more content for the game, and help pay for servers and other architecture for maintaining the gameplay experience online for months and years to come. Once released, if the players can reengage with the game every few months with new content, it not only brings them back in but new players as well who learn about the newest update and cool content for a title they didn't have the time and money for just a few months earlier. The industry moves so fast, and there is just so many games available that any ability to be noticed is pounced on. So, what are the other ways that can be used to generate more money?

DLC

DLC or Downloadable Content is made from all sorts of additions and changes, some resembling cosmetic changes from Free to Play content all the way to huge gameplay additions that add dozens or even hundreds of gameplay hours to the original offering. The pricing also scales based on the amount of content in the DLC and can be cheap for only a few dollars compared to the cost of an entirely new game. The biggest criticism of DLC is "Why didn't they just include this with the main game?". The implication is that the creators "held back" content just so they could sell it to the players at a later date, essentially purposely making an inferior game so they could profit twice. Having shipped many games over the years, let me tell you, we barely get what is in the box on time. In my career as a games maker, I have never, ever had the luxury of sitting on finished, fun, and "ready to go" content ahead of the release date on any game. This includes small teams working on passion projects to mega franchises such as *Call of Duty* with hundreds of people. Publishers and shareholders may be that "greedy", but developers don't have that kind of bandwidth to pull off the amount of content even if that was the initial plan.

Subscriptions

This used to be a monetisation method reserved for games with persistent online components, mainly Massively Multiplayer Online games such as *World of Warcraft*; however, some game makers have tried this on other genres and game types. In essence, players are charged a small flat fee per month, quarter, or year that enables content they would not normally have access. Sometimes the entire game was put behind this paywall.

Most recently first-person shooter games such as *Call of Duty* and the *Battlefield* series have tried out a subscription service but called it a "Season Pass". Essentially a yearly fee, players would receive any new content (DLC) as a part of the subscription price. In addition to this content, they would get boosts, advantages, and even features that would otherwise be unavailable to those who don't subscribe. The subscription fee would be less expensive than buying all the content separately in theory—basically a purchase by the player on the promise of compelling content in the future. Creators get the money up front. Due to the negative experiences by players and missteps by content providers justifying the extra cost of season passes, this method is dying out and exists mainly in a few remaining online only games.

Virtual and Augmented Reality: Are we there yet? How about now? Now?

Screaming—actual screaming was my introduction to VR. It was not a subtle or nuanced scream, but a throaty, fully felt primal exultation of terror. It thankfully wasn't me making all the noise, I was still in "real" reality but the user (whom will remain nameless for dignity reasons and owes me a pint) was experiencing something every bit as factual to him as my "real" reality was experienced by me. There is something incredibly magical when you are sitting in Ferrari 458 Italia on a racetrack, getting ready to race as the tension builds. Looking around the car, checking the mirrors, you glance over to a friend in a matching car next to you and taunt "good luck" sarcastically in the voice coms just before the lights change to signal the start of the race. Pinning the accelerator with the melodious, yet angry scream of the Ferrari, the engine bursts to life and launches towards the race of your life. In reality, you're in underwear on the couch with a Sony PS VR headset on but could pass a polygraph test that day, swearing up and down having raced a real Ferrari. It's that amazing.

The latest launch of the Virtual Reality trend was a public push beginning with Oculus Rift in 2014. Starting as an idea and a crowdfunding campaign, to the Oculus got into people's minds that the concept of virtual reality as an actual product could exist. This is not the first time that VR was "just around the corner". Back in 1995/1996 at BioWare, we were looking at some specific hardware. Movies like *The Lawnmower Man* and others made it look all too easy, but the hardware was heavy, slow, and very, very low resolution. Back in the day when 640 x 480 displays were standard, VR looked even more "potato": a helmet that weighed multiple pounds and had screens looking like a bad monitor a few feet in front of you, while in the end an actual bad monitor just a few feet in front of you was the better option. The technology was just not there to support this compelling idea. A few attempts were made by manufactures, small ones mostly, and they all failed. Outside of a university, the military, or a few tech companies, most people could not realy find an experience that did not cost hundreds of thousands, if not millions, of dollars. Before we dip in any further, let's get some basic definitions out of the way.

What is VR?

Virtual Reality, or VR, is usually applied to the experience where a user's reality, what they see, hear, and experience, is completely replaced by a world created from the program and hardware. Usually it's provided by goggles, glasses, or some form of helmet where there are screens in front of the user that completely blocks out the "real" outside world (in the case of Samsung Gear VR, the headset uses a phone as the screen). For complete suspension of disbelief, techniques like motion tracking are utilized (the world moves when the user's head moves, etc.). It does not feel like a window into another world but more a complete replacement, total immersion.

When firing up a VR game to play, you are IN the game. You are the character in the scenario. If you walk around the environment, it looks and feels as if you are actually there and present.

Think of it as visiting a fantasy world.

What is AR?

Augmented Reality, or AR, is different from VR in that this technology projects a false reality on top of actual reality, usually expressed as holograms and audio enhancement into the user's world.

When firing up any program, the experience is in your current environment, taking into account the surroundings. Players can walk around projected "things" and react as if they were actually present.

Think of it as a fantasy world visiting you.

Why do we care?

There are shifts in technology and how we use it every few years. 3D video cards became affordable in the late 1990s, creating a major shift in games and culture, and special effects really took off in movies and TV because of the cheap access to both the hardware and software. The next big shift was in the mid-2000s with the mass adoption of mobile phone technology and creation of a huge new user base. People that did traditionally fit into the gamer mould but did not consider themselves gamers were playing *Candy Crush Saga* or *Angry Birds*. These people in fact were the hundred millions of new gamers using powerful hardware in their pockets and handbags. This created another shift in mindsets and how we interact with our world: constantly in contact, tracked, able to navigate virtually the entire knowledge base of humanity at any time, and able to distract ourselves at a whim.

VR/AR is yet another step forward, while keeping in mind every step we took with technology was not linear in scale or importance. If 3D was a big step forward into making digital worlds look real, mobile technology put gaming in our hands and made comfort using it universal which was more important than the previous step of 3D. VR/AR could be the quantum leap beyond either of those. The preceding technologies were prerequisites both in the actual technology itself, but also socially and culturally to make this next step even possible.

With large tech companies such as Facebook, Google, Microsoft, and most phone companies (Samsung, Apple, HTC), and even big gaming names like Valve investing billions of dollars into this new frontier, something exciting will shake out. Will this be another 1995 false start? I don't think so, too many of the old hurdles have been conquered in other elements and industries, I think we have turned the corner, and if we want VR/AR to be part of our lives, it will be so.

So really... what's different now?

First off, display technology has moved an incredible amount, both in resolution and power consumption. A large part is due to the consumer electronics around us. Our smartphones and tablets have done more for the forward momentum of technology than anyone could have imagined. What the two world wars did for technological advances (computers, encryption, plastics, rocketry, and robots), we are now seeing in consumer demand and corporate profitability as a driving force. Both paths to technological advancement are kind of scary to be honest. At any rate, the screens or optics were the real first hurdle. No point in making a device, no matter how big or small, when the result can't support text or even basic quality of graphics that we have all come to expect.

Second is an incredible increase in computing power. Moore's law[1] and all that jazz. Although closely linked to the increase in optics viability, the part of VR/AR that many people seem to underestimate are the components outside the projectors or screens in front of your eyes. Motion tracking, higher resolution, small cameras, room scanning, voice activation, and gesture interpretation

---

[1] Observation made in 1965 by Gordon Moore, co-founder of Intel, that the number of transistors per square inch on integrated circuits had doubled every year since the integrated circuit was invented. This has continued since, which is incredible.

are serious bits of software and hardware that make any VR/AR experience work and require real computing horsepower. In the case of Microsoft's HoloLens, all these key components are onboard with the processing power in a headset weighing only a few hundred grams. This feat of technology was plain impossible even a few years ago. Now is the first time these elements can come together and legitimately create, if not now then very soon, a consumer level device that can meet the original dream of VR/AR.

Lastly is the social element. 20 years ago, computers were scary to most people. "What if I break it?" is the question I would hear from technophobes unwilling to even touch computers, afraid to "do something wrong", let alone explore and get the most out of the hardware. As a rule, hardware was expensive, uncommon, and meant for "work". Current technology makes those computers look positively silly in their lack of functionality, and more importantly are so ubiquitous that you honestly don't even realise how integrated it is in our society. Go on, how far away is the nearest item with at least one microprocessor? Look at any phone, tablet, computer, most watches, thermostats, cars, etc. Most have internet access, and those that don't will in the next few years. Parents now use technology without effort, modern offices could not function without computers, and most people under the age of 18 have never lived in a world without them seeming so unexceptional as to be unnoticed. This just wasn't the case 20 years ago when the first push for VR happened. Now on the cusp of having this technology, this is the logical next step, going through a door other technology has opened for the masses already. At first it will stand out in public like a mobile phone did in 1990, and like mobile phones now, this technology will disappear from our collective consciousness as standing out. They just "are".

What does VR actually "give" us?

AR/VR is one of those experiences that is difficulty to describe, almost impossible to get across the actual experience. Never has "you had to be there" as an expression been so apt. The level of immersion—whatever experience the program is providing—is so complete, so "real" compared to looking at a 2D screen and totally convincing. Your sense of presence changes what the technology can convey and how it can be used.

While in a virtual theatre watching a movie, the person is in a theatre, almost expecting sticky floors and the AC making the space uncomfortably cold. More active experiences such as flying a plane or driving a car, things recognised from real life, seem totally believable as happening: leaning into corners in your race car, feeling vertigo looking down from your plane when banking, and other amazing, "being there" experiences.

Then there are the fantastical things you could never do in the real world. People can walk around on the surface of Mars using NASA data or operate a giant robot and level a city with friends. It's the presence that makes the experience so unique and amazing.

There are genres of games that may not be so good because of this immersion. Horror games, especially with "jump scares", are just cruel. When staring at something scary on a 2D monitor or screen, your brain knows it's not real. There is a hurdle in the suspension of disbelief, which although makes most experiences less believable, also serves as a layer of protection for others. When that monster or other threat jumps out in VR, your brain cannot distinguish that it's not real. It seems very real, the fight or flight response kicks in and not necessarily in a " ha, ha, that was thrilling" kind of way. More like heart attack inducing real.

What are the current drawbacks?

The technology, both hardware and software, is not perfected yet. Far from it, we are still in the very early stages. VR/AR has come a long way in the last 12 months, but there are inherent flaws that have yet to be sorted yet. The biggest one is that some people get a feeling of nausea nicknamed "VR sickness". What someone sees and hears when using the technology sends signals to the brain indicating actual physical movement. The inner ear and every other part of the body is telling conflicting information, that in fact you are nOT doing a loop de loop in an airplane currently. This disagreement between the senses can make someone feel rather ill and hit after a few minutes, hours, or never at all. I am lucky enough not to be affected, but I think my wife, who gets ill just watching me play first-person shooters on a standard projector, would not fare so well. This will have to be solved as making a measurable percentage of users physically ill is not suitable for advertising on posters. Rest assured, very intelligent people are working on this, and it will get solved as every other technological problem... eventually.

Something else to keep in mind is that some VR is "room-scale", where the game or experience takes place in a virtual room players can move around. This is how some of the most compelling experiences in VR are done, but they actually require real space in a house, office or wherever someone is planning to play. To avoid smashing a lamp or tripping on a chair, you need to make space. Not everyone can set aside 1.5 m by 2 m (5 ft by 6.5 ft) for gaming space which is the minimum suggested. The days of gaming exclusively while sitting in a chair or on a couch are numbered.

Another drawback of VR (but not AR) is that the very act of using it cuts off the player from their environment. It's the point but also not conducive to traditional social interaction. Someone may want to watch an IMAX movie on the couch by popping on the VR, but everyone else can't participate even if they are sitting literally together. At this point, most people won't be talking or interacting with anyone while using VR, unless they are also in VR and connected to the same activity. I am looking forward to sitting in a theatre with all my friends from all over the world, watching something at the same time and hanging out. Odd that my wife could be sitting right next to me in the real world and not be able to participate in the experience. This is a social thing and good reason why the television or monitor may not be going anywhere and certainly not be replaced by VR tech. There will be different ways to experience events and entertainment as now, but VR will be added to the list of possibilities.

Sounds great! I am in: Getting into the industry

How I got into the industry

Back in the early 1990s when I attended high school in Grande Prairie, Alberta—no wait, this starts even earlier. I remember when my dad brought home that Atari 2600 for Christmas. Games like *Space Invaders*, PAC-MAN and *Defender* ruled my free time for many years. I also remember quite clearly my dad taking me to his office and letting me play *King's Quest* on his work PC for hours on end in the early 1980s while he did other things. In case you never played the original *King's Quest*, imagine a text adventure but with rudimentary graphics, brutally tough logic puzzles, and no way to get help if you were stuck since there was no internet to find walkthroughs or anything else for that matter. Best game ever. Never finished it.

Now imagine the excitement I had when he brought home that old office computer for us to use whenever we wanted. Truly a highpoint in my gaming life, it was a PC XT by IBM, (Intel 8086 for the more tech-minded and old enough to remember this PC). This computer had a CGA graphics card and PC speaker, and you had to fiddle with the *Autoexec.bat* and *Config.sys* system files every time to run something new. Mobile phones now have 10,000 times more processing power than the XT, but to me at that time, the PC may as well been on a pedestal with white light beaming and angelic choirs singing whenever I looked at it. The basement was its home and resting place, much like my free time and youth.

One of my fondest memories of gaming was the *Advanced Dungeons and Dragons: Gold Box* series. Each game came on 3.5¼ disks labelled "A" ,"B" and "C", and players used a little code wheel to decipher characters that appeared on the screen for copy protection. I saved up my money for weeks and months to buy these games, and I am sure that if you worked out the cost per minute of entertainment it is close to $0.01 per day. Save a child in Africa from starvation or keep a kid from causing mischief on the streets of Canada for a few months. I stand by my choice.

The game took forever to load on my machine. Seriously, I would insert the first disk (after playing with *Config.sys* and *Autoexec.bat* for a while to make it work), and grab a sandwich and glass of milk, call a friend, etc. Eventually it would ask for "disk B". Repeat process. It was worth it. I even had a few friends that would come over and help me map out where everything was in the game while I played. There were riddles, mazes, and lots of combat to keep a player busy. Even cooler was that the game used the *AD&D* system, the very system we used to play the pen and paper game. It was like being able to play *D&D* anytime you wanted, even if your Dungeon Master had homework or was grounded. Role-playing nirvana. You could create an entire party from scratch, use all the classes, spells, and *D&D* items you wanted and choosing how they looked (well, within a 16 x 16 pixel animated stick figure). It was a truly an ambitious game.

The other big moment was years later, and a few PC upgrades in-between, when I bought a sound card from Creative Labs, a Sound Blaster. To this day, I do not recall how I convinced my dad to buy the sound card, but I needed it for one game, *DOOM*. Maybe it was the crazed look in my eyes, the gamer's equivalent to "crack eyes" that made him do it. Maybe he was afraid I would knock over a liquor store for the cash. At any rate, the card was purchased and installed, transforming to computer +1.

It all started like this: I was over at a friend's house, and he had the shareware version of *DOOM*. Within 10 seconds I realized gaming had changed forever. I had played *Blake Stone: Aliens of Gold* and *Castle Wolfenstein* (loved it!), but *DOOM* was different—

scary, dark, and with demons! As a teenager, you need nothing else. The sound and graphics were so far beyond anything at the time that it was like showing cavemen a missile launcher. No idea how it works, but sure is cool. For added effect, turn off the lights and up the sound, and within minutes of cacodemons roars and you screaming there would be stomping on the floor from upstairs followed by "What the hell are you doing down there!?" mother call.

The summary is basically I had always been a gamer, but I had no idea how to get into the games industry even though I wanted to be a part of it.

During high school in Grande Prairie, a small group of us—Cam Tofer, Marcia Olsen, Dean Andersen, and myself—hung out together both in and out of school. I met Cam from computer class where he was causing all sorts of havoc with the teacher because he clearly knew more about programming or computers than anyone in the building. He had pretty much free reign there, and due to his disruptive nature, we got along famously. He was dating Marcia, a very talented artist in her own right, and I met Dean through mutual friends and had played *AD&D* together for years. Dean was a great artist and a wicked rogue in our pen and paper campaign. Cam was the unofficial leader, as what we could and could not do was based on what code he could create. During class one day, we decided to make our own roleplaying game. Since I could not code as well as Cam, which is a gross understatement, and my artistic skills were negligible, it fell onto me to come up with the design and work with the others to try putting the game together. It was a simple 2D isometric[1] RPG with its own rule system that I created. We had a functioning level with basic controls and some cool 2D layering effects, etc., around the time we all graduated from high school, and needed to get jobs and be ready for college in the fall. What it really meant is that we went to Cam's family farmhouse and stayed in the attic for days on end working, writing, and coding. Work and school were second—a distant second—so distant that if we didn't get into the games industry, we would have been in big trouble. There were a few distractions, and we made a rule that *Sid Meyer's Civilization* was not allowed on anyone's computer. About this time, we met Cass Scott, a 3D artist/modeller that was a breath of fresh air into the group.

---

[1] Isometric projection is a method for showing three-dimensional objects in 2D. Three coordinate axes appear equally foreshortened, and the angle between any two is 120 degrees. Basically the 'camera' or viewpoint is raised above the scene and pushed to the side in a ¾ view, giving a god-like overview and the illusion of 3D depth.

In the fall of 1995, one of Cam's friends, another programmer and musician who was at the University of Alberta, had heard of a company called BioWare starting up in Edmonton. After a few tentative discussions with Ray Muzyka, we all agreed to go down and meet them. We convinced James Ohlen (who will pop up again later in this book to drive us the 500 kilometres in his beat-up station wagon, full with computers, and 5+ people in -30 degree weather down to Edmonton. You know we grew up in the middle of nowhere north when driving "down" to Edmonton, Alberta, Canada.

We had no idea what to expect. BioWare was new, they had not shipped anything nor had we heard of them, but they wanted to talk to us. Any chance to see other people doing similar things as us was well worth the trip.

This was when BioWare was located on top of a coffee shop by the University of Alberta. It was a beat-up old place but who were we to judge—we were working out of a farmhouse attic! I had never been so nervous, but we all sat down to talk, and when gamers talk to gamers, it's all good. Three doctors founded the company just a few months before: Ray Muzyka, Greg Zeschuk, and Augustine Yip. They had just got out of medical school, started practicing medicine, and realized not only did they love games, but banks would give doctors loans! The current BioWare team had Russ Rice and Dan

Walker, two awesome artists, and Scott Greig, their lead programmer.

We fired up our demo, and I handed over my design docs for our game. They looked them over, talked for a bit, then we all went out for lunch at Pharos Pizza, just down the block from the office (the first of many, many pizzas in my career). They were genuinely great people, and as we ate, the desire to work with them grew over that lunch until it was nearly unbearable. When we returned to the office, they showed us their project, *Battleground Infinity*, a isometric 2D RPG. "What a perfect fit!" I was thinking. They were in the middle of pitching it to pretty much every publisher and had no deals yet but were hopeful. To fill in the gap, they took over development of a game called *Shattered Steel* for a developer in Calgary called Pyrotech. From Pyrotech they inherited Trent Oster and Jon Winski, a producer and a programmer that had long and successful careers at BioWare. *Shattered Steel* was going to be published by Interplay, and BioWare was hopeful to sign the RPG as well.

It was a long drive home, even for 500+ kilometre in a Canadian blizzard. BioWare said they would call us, and it all hinged on getting *Battleground Infinity* signed with a publisher. Those were painful weeks of waiting and working. We talked to them a few times (more like harassed really) over the next weeks trying to get an update, because quite honestly the waiting was beyond painful. We were so close to working on an actual game.

We finally got the call! "Come down again so we can talk." We headed down to Edmonton again, this time to work out the details of hiring the lot of us. There were some changes and requests. One of the first things they asked was "If you come down and work for us, you would have to put your game on the shelf and work only on *Battleground*". Thinking all of 0.2 of a second, we agreed. The second thing BioWare asked is if we could bring our own machines, and they would buy them off us once the project was signed. Again a no brainer, we preferred it, and had recently bought ourselves beefy P75 machines a few months before and were quite proud. It took a while for this to all sink in. BioWare, a game company, was actually going to pay us to do what we did for fun!

There was much upheaval over the next few months as we dropped out of school, quit jobs, and generally pulled up stake and moved from our little northern community to the bustling capital of Alberta, Edmonton. For some of us, it was not so easy to tell our parents and loved ones: "Ya, you know I was going into law school. Well, I quit and am now going to make video games."

Insert stunned silence here.

In all honesty, our families as a whole were quite supportive, but I think deep down they all thought it was just a phase, and we would be back in school in a year after it all went pear-shaped. I think to their surprise BioWare took off in ways no one could have imagined at that early stage.

Summary of the whole story is this: we loved games, we played games, and we grouped together to make a game. This is one of the most reliable ways to get into the industry. Mod groups do it all the time, proving they can make games by actually making a game. A demo, proof of concept, anything to put you ahead of the masses who want a job because they like the idea of making games.

But seriously, how do I get into the games industry?

"How does one get into games?" This is one of the most often asked questions I get from people outside the industry. From friends who don't like their jobs to schools I have presented at, this is invariably the kick-off question that I get asked. It's a natural place to start the conversation.

The sad truth is, there is no one answer. There is a large degree of luck and timing involved. Probably not something you wanted to hear if looking for a fool proof way to get in. You need to be driven and willing to work insane hours, paying your dues just like any other industry. You may also not start out doing exactly what you wanted, but your foot will be in the door and moving closer towards your goal.

This also assumes you are talented, intelligent, and work well with teams. Take a close look on why you want to join the gaming industry. During my talks at places such as the Vancouver Film

School, I make it very clear that as an artist, they are a production artist with a certain amount of time to do work, and believe me, it's always less than ideal. Companies are flexible to some extent for personality types, skill sets, etc., but bottom line, employees need to get concepts/models/textures/levels done regardless if someone feels particularly "creative" that day or not. There is no overtime, it's just called a workday. It can be 16+ hours during crunch time and last weeks, if not months. When starting in the industry, workers are not paid particularly well, and even once the game is done, don't expect to get rich or become a rock star. To be in this industry, must must really want to make games: love them, breath them, and want to be part of a creative team that gives the fun back to the gamers. You remember playing games as a kid and loving them, and want to contribute that feeling for others. Sounds crazy, but it's what drives many when the pressure gets high.

But how do you get into the industry?

Method One: Make something more than a resume

As I described above, making a demo that works from concept to execution will prove to a company, whether publisher or a developer, that you can complete something. One developer that I worked with relatively recently that used a demo to break into the industry was Splash Damage. The studio worked on *Quake* mods, eventually making *Wolfenstien:Enemy Territory*, followed by *DOOM 3* and *Enemy Territory: Quake Wars*. Currently Splash Damage is working on their own titles and technology. All of this started with a handful of people creating something they loved using other people's tech and know-how as a launching point.

Splash Damage started scattered all over the world and did not join together as a "company" until after several projects and years. Their success is based on delivering actual games that people could play and enjoy. Once you have a track record, many doors open. With mobile development and being able to publish on places like the Apple App store, game makers can have a huge reach very easily to show off their skills.

There are so many ways now to make your talents known, heard, and seen. Blogs, fan sites, and message boards are great venues to display designs, demo reels, or even full projects. People "in the know" visit these places regularly looking for talent, and in amongst thousands of half-baked ideas, there are always diamonds in the rough that stand out. Showing commitment and drive for quality in the site and its content will reflect directly on the first impression a prospective employer will have of you and by association, your work. In the FPS genre, this is actually easier than in most others.

Engines and tools are available all over the place and often free. There are also large communities to join, share ideas, and receive feedback. A great place to find like-minded people and start larger projects, the skill sets vary widely so you will always find someone to learn from or work with.

Setting up a webpage or blog that not only covers your work but also other peoples' work that you enjoy, including professionals, is a great way to get website traffic. I have hired fan site people for not just community manager type roles but as designers and level designers, programmers, and artists.

Going to trade shows, assuming you live close to one or can get there, is another way to make contact as there are often job fairs, plus dev people keep their eyes open for new talent. Many of these have venues show off indie projects and talent, and again is an overall great place to network.

Method Two: Join a publisher or developer as QA

Publishers especially hire students with little or no experience to help test games. Many people have used this as the launching pad into production, design, programming, and art. It gets you on the radar, above the masses that want the job. It also provides an inside look into the industry and may help shape the direction in which you want to go. The major drawback is needing to be close to an existing publisher or developer. If living in the middle of nowhere (like I did), this option may not be open to you.

These entry-level jobs are often low paying and tedious, and have long hours and no glory in doing them; however, this experience provides a broad appreciation for what goes into making games and if you are smart, willing, and determined, this is absolutely a way into the industry. To be honest, 99% of making games is in fact tedious, long hours, and without glory, so it really is a crash course in what lies ahead.

Publishers hire in waves depending on need and can fluctuate greatly throughout the year; this is especially true for the lead up to the Christmas push. Christmas launches really start in September, which means with the submissions and first party sign-offs (Sony, Microsoft, Nintendo, etc), these games must be in Alpha and QA for the spring to guarantee being on the shelves for consumers in fall. During this time between April and September, publisher QA headcounts can grow from a few dozen long-term employees and managers to many hundreds just to ensure that these games hit their ship dates and the lucrative Christmas rush.

During this time, the demand for QA often outstrips the supply and sometimes seems that they will hire anyone with a heartbeat.

Now this is obviously an exaggeration, but I have met QA folks who look like extras from a *Mad Max* film with all the social graces and hygiene skills to match. Of course, I have also met highly articulate, intelligent, and informed people as well, and those are the people that move up rather quickly in the ranks, either managing and leading QA, or moving into other areas. The point is that the spring and summer are a great time to hit up publishers for entry-level position.

Method Three: Be stunningly talented

Another way of being above the crowd is to be amazingly talented at what you do. From writing white papers to having art shows, if you have the talent, people will find you. This is a bit harder for a designer or producer, as without something "solid" to show, convincing people of your skills is difficult. We are talking about the top 1% of people in the industry, and the odds are, it's not you. Don't worry, games are not made by rock stars but by the 99% of hard working and dedicated people who master their craft. Those 1% are important, they help drive innovation or create a flavour for a project, but the fact is that teams on big games number in the hundreds, and knowing your skills and weaknesses, and delivering work on time will help get a foot in the door.

Method Four: Get an education

This is becoming more and more a route to get into the industry, but I still list it nearly last. I would hire someone with two years' experience shipping one decent mod over someone who has tons of schooling but has no idea what he/she is getting into. Schooling is a great way to improve base skills followed by working on getting yourself noticed by creating something. There are many bright people out there, and finishing a computer science degree does not in itself pull someone above; however, the final project made while in those courses can and will put you ahead of others. Education alone is only one aspect of consideration, which I weight lower than experience personally. This also differs depending on the company, needs, and position. Generally for programming and similar, education is far more relevant than a design or production type position.

Also, keep in mind that the games industry is not just artists and programmers. We need economists, marketing people, lawyers, and anything else a well-rounded business would need to function, especially in larger companies. I love working with people at game companies that are gamers themselves, we are all one happy family trying to make the best games possible. Sharing that enthusiasm no matter what role for the project makes a great work environment and better games.

I have worked with people from academia on projects with mixed results. Knowing the theory is one thing but another when implementing it with imperfect tech and limited time while still making something good: the difference between "in theory" and " in practice". Taking the best from both worlds is needed to deliver great things, and school usually only focuses on and/or teaches theory or application. Add that there are far more students graduating every year than positions in the industry, and many find more than a degree is needed to stand out and be noticed.

Method Five: Know someone

This is very person specific, but I have seen more than a few people bring their friends into entry level positions within companies. These are not just random folks they happen to know. In general, we befriend people with similar likes, tastes, and pastimes. We gravitate towards people like us: if I code games, I probably have coder friends. This happens in smaller companies and start-ups more now than anywhere else, and less as the industry matures. This is mostly likely not that useful and akin to luck, but you may be surprised at the number of folks that have an "in" into the games industry if you look around.

A note about women making games

Females are sadly underrepresented in most aspects in making games. In an average developer, there is the odd female artist, maybe a designer. I have only ever worked with two female programmers in my career. In production, the numbers increase slightly, but overall, I would say in my 20+ years of making games that females made up less than 10% of any team. In publishing the numbers increase quite a bit and are closer to 30-40% but in roles involved in the business of making games rather than making games: marketing, PR, sales, production, legal, etc. . There are two main reasons why:

1) People tend to work in industries they like and are exposed to.

Until quite recently. games were made with little regard (in most cases) in appealing to a female audience. If you never played a video game, when choosing a career path, game maker wouldn't even occur. This is changing now since everyone is exposed to video games. No longer is a high-end PC or spending hundreds of dollars on a console required for gaming, which were huge barriers assuming there is a game available that you would enjoy. In fact,

99% of people reading this have a decent gaming system in their pocket. This exposure via mobile phones and the like has opened-up the field to a larger group of gamers that will one day join our ranks in game making.

2) Until recently the prerequisite degrees and perception of the industry in general has not actively targeted female participation.

Computer science, engineering, and mathematics are the most common degrees for people in the industry, but females are five times less likely to consider a technology related career. This has nothing to do with actual aptitude or skill. The very first programmers were female, people like Ada Lovelace and Grace Hopper—it is completely societal bias and thinking, and thankfully is changing, albeit slowly.

The more well-rounded the team is, whether gender, race, religion, or any other aspect of life, the better off the team and for that matter, the game will be better. Disparate experience not only helps make better games, but also helps us understand the people who will be playing the game better, appealing to the positive and diverse aspects of their lives that we would otherwise not have inside knowledge.

There are many ways to get into the gaming industry, but the best way is to do something—get involved and start hanging out in game creator circles online. Mix with other creative and driven people. Opportunity may rely on luck, but I found the more exposure, the more actively involved, the more "luck" you create. I have created my own opportunities far more than they have been handed to me or just fell into my lap.

Endrant: The birth, life, and death of an indie studio

One of the best ways to get some insight into the industry is reading about the birth of a studio, shipping a product, and subsequent death of the same studio. Endrant was a game development studio I started along with my business partner, Neil Postlethwaite. Although a tumultuous and often heart-wrenching ride overall, this was a great learning experience in aspects that until that point I had only observed second hand.

After *Enemy Territory: Quake Wars* shipped in 2008, a new developer came into being, my company Endrant Studios. Saying it was "mine" is a bit strong. I was Co-owner and Creative Director, but the driving force for the studio was the team itself (as with every studio really). How it started was quite simple: we saw an opening and took it. Below is a fuller account of the birth and death of an indie studio.

Inception

I had been working at Activision as a producer and creative director since 2001, focusing mainly on first-person shooters. My first project was *Soldier of Fortune II: Double Helix*; I joined late and worked mostly on multiplayer and localisation. This position was my inaugural exposure first-hand into publishing, and I could not have asked for better mentors, projects, or people to work with—the aforementioned 4710 group. We fell under Mark Lamia and Laird Malamed's team in one form or another, and it was a tight crew. Games such as *Call of Duty*, *Star Wars: Jedi Knight*, *DOOM*, *Quake 3*, and *Wolfenstein*, plus the *Star Trek* games fell into this group. We loved what we were doing and making great games.

Fast forward a few years. I found myself working on *Enemy Territory: Quake Wars* as the Creative Director onsite with the developer Splash Damage for 3½ years. During this time, I built up a great relationship with id Software, the IP and tech holders. id Software is famous for basically creating the first-person shooter genre, and what they said went in any project related to their studio. It was a collaborative effort and good relationship between the three shareholders, but in particular, Kevin Cloud from id Software, Paul Wedgewood of Splash Damage, and I spent a lot of time arguing over all sorts of things from game direction to how much damage a sniper rifle should do—it was fantastic. id Software and Activision's relationship had ups and downs, and certainly demanded the utmost care and attention from everyone. Being from a developer background, I completely understood why id Software made certain requests, and now from the publisher angle I could actually see why things were being a specific way. Demonstrating that I was more than just another person from the publisher in order to gain the necessary trust and freedom to become the Creative Director took time to prove. Once proving I only cared about the fun and quality of the game, we got along famously.

Right around the end of the project in 2007, I looked into what was next in the Activision pipeline that I could work on and one title kept popping up: *Wolfenstein*, an id Software IP that would be made using the studio's proprietary technology. The project had been struggling for a long while, and specifically multiplayer had been passed from developer to developer without gaining traction. I was sitting with Laird, who was in charge of 4710 by that time, talking about the project one day. We were trying to figure out what was needed, and where to find a dev that id Software would trust and could actually deliver the game, and a thought struck me. I could do this. Now I didn't have a dev team per se, but I did know a few key people that were looking around and talking about maybe doing a new project.

The first step was to figure out if this was a flight of fancy or actually possible . Neil Postlethwaite, the Managing Director of Splash Damage, was one of those people looking for a new challenge, and over the years we had become fast friends. Over coffee (as most of these initial meetings were held) I brought up the opportunity, and we discussed becoming partners and maybe chasing this pipe dream. We had to figure out what needed to be done and who would be key in making this possible. A Creative Director and a Managing Director does not a developer make. We looked at all the folks we knew that were either available or looking to leave their current positions, concluding "This may actually be possible!". We had to be very careful with some of these people since we did not want our actual "invitation" be the deciding factor if someone was leaving their current positions. What I am dancing around is that many of Endrant's founding members, the key folks that made *Wolfenstein* even possible, were from Splash Damage, the dev Neil and I were currently working at. This had to be done properly as neither of us wanted to hurt Splash Damage; the company was full of great people making great things, and they were our friends and comrades.

There were two conversations needing to happen, neither I was particularly looking forward to but necessary to . The first was with Laird: pitching him the idea of me leaving Activision after eight years, starting a developer studio, and walking into the *Wolfenstein* contract. On top of that we were looking for a small investment up front alongside the meagre funds we raised so we could start at full pace rather than a slow ramp-up. I could not even meet face-to-face, time was pressing and he was back in the Santa Monica office while I was in London, so it was a phone call. "Hey Laird, here is a crazy thought—you let me know how crazy. You know how we are looking for a developer for *Wolfenstein* Multiplayer? What if I started that developer and did that for you?" He hardly paused at all and replied, "That is not crazy at all, and if it doesn't work out you always can come back to us at ATVI." I was overjoyed once I got over the initial shock of how easy the conversation had been since I had prepared for the worst. Business plans, pitches, and other aspects had to be worked out, but at least we knew that Activision was open to discussions. As well, we needed another discussion out of the way first, and if it did not go well could end the studio in its tracks.

The second discussion was with Paul Wedgewood, the owner and CEO of Splash Damage. We could not in good conscious start a new company, working on an IP Splash Damage worked on in the

288

past with many of our leads former (some current) SD employees. This step was the most precarious and stressful as this could go very badly. Paul had a great relationship with id software too, and could scuttle this before it even starts if he felt betrayed or even perceived us slighting him. Even if he didn't go that route, he could make the creation of the new studio very painful in uncountable other ways. Heck, we could end up in a fist fight on the spot (unlikely but not impossible). In front of the Splash Damage offices I often went with Paul for a cigarette (I don't smoke, but it was a good time to talk with Paul about various topics without distraction). I laid out the studio plan, project, and the fact that some of his former and current team members wanted to join. I also made clear even if this did not go forward, those same team members were going to leave SD—I was just giving them a place to land. I stressed we were not headhunting through SD for people, sign whatever he wanted for a non-compete, and never hire (or even talk to) anyone currently working at SD without going through Paul first. Now Paul could have gone a lot of different ways with this. Over the years we had become friends. I would tip a pint with him without hesitation in any situation, but this was hitting awfully close to home, and no matter his response I could not fault him.

After a silence and careful consideration, he started asking about the project and how we were setting up the studio, and then dropped "Do you need any investment?" Honestly I was shocked, relieved, happy, and relieved again at how he viewed my proposal. Paul realized we were not threatening or actively hurting him or Splash Damage, and knew we never would—we were friends. We honestly worked too hard with Paul and his team to help make their games. We never took up Paul on the investment offer and kept true to our promise of never hiring away anyone from Splash Damage. Second step done.

With the core members lined up, Paul's blessing, and Laird's consent, it was time to put this studio together.

Birth

So how do you even start a developer as an entity? You hire accountants, register at Companies House if you are in the UK, and partake in a host of other things any company needs to officially "exist". I won't bore you with those details, but we still had a few very serious hurdles to cross before starting proper development:

1) We still had huge holes in our staff line-up.
2) We did not have the contract yet.
3) We had limited start-up capital.

These three items basically all interlinked with each other and made solving each individually quite difficult.

First thing to solve was the contract. Without the work guarantee on the game from Activision, there was no way to move forward. We could not secure working space, loans, or anything else without at least a letter of intent (which is just a few pages saying "Yes, we are negotiating in good faith for a contract worth about '$X USD' signed by Activision and us). The existing relationship with Activision helped a great deal. Considering we were technically starting "cold", I could not involve them in any discussions until after Endrant was officially a company and the founders (including myself) were separated from previous responsibilities.

We got the letter of intent within a few weeks and used it to secure temporary working space in Sevenoaks, UK, a small village just south of London, close to where a bunch of us lived next to a train station. The office was small, lacked AC, and barely fit our purpose, but it was ours. There was a feeling of the initial BioWare experience, which was nostalgic for me. More importantly, Endrant officially existed.

Next we were off to IKEA for desks and other cheap as possible office supplies. There were only seven of us at the start with a whole lot to accomplish. Actual contract negotiations were in full swing, and Activision was sending us console development kits simultaneously as time was tight. The contract itself was very simple: *Wolfenstien* was to be more or less a "work for hire" contract with the promise of a bigger and better project afterwards. Work for hire is basically we work for milestone payments, own nothing, receive nothing after the game ships beyond bonuses based on meeting dates, and earn an extra amount for Metacritic average scores, etc. This deal was the quintessential "pay your dues" project, and boy, were we about to discover the "pay" part of that statement.

We were in contact with headhunters, and putting out feelers to friends and former co-workers, hoping to find talented folks that would help fill our ranks. We had all the lead positions filled, but we needed artists, animators, programmers, and other roles. Now it is not so easy to hire talented people and preferably those with experience when starting a new company. The message to prospective employees is that "Yes, we have a decent sized contract on a big IP and our founders have 100+ years combined experience, but this is still a risk". I think that when interviewees showed up at our temporary offices they got the message we were a start-up. We hired around 15 people, plus a few contractors very quickly to give Endrant a chance to complete the game on time. We got rather lucky with the folks we hired, some real talented and great people.

The Project

As I mentioned before, we were not the first developer on *Wolfenstien* multiplayer. In fact the three different versions—Xbox360, PS3, and PC—had been worked on by different teams with three different codebases[1] in various states of disarray. Add in that the single player was being done by Raven Software (owned by Activision), and the studio was behind schedule, still making decisions and changes to the game constantly which became a moving target to deliver the game (think golf except the holes move after each swing). Oh, did I mention Raven Software was on yet another codebase.

We had less than a year for sorting, shipping, and translating into a dozen plus languages simultaneously while delivering the game on all three platforms. The first thing we did was fly to Wisconsin where Raven Software is located and had marathon meetings to get up to speed: what they were working on, what they

---

[1] A codebase is a version of the underlying computer code for the engine that the game runs on, in our case id Tech. Having different versions means that essentially any work had to be recreated for each version, and is a costly and terrible expenditure of time to keep changes in sync, which is constantly hundreds of times a day.

were planning, and any major things we should avoid. I had worked indirectly with them while working with Activision so I knew a few folks there, which definitely helped. Overall Raven Software had a decent plan, realizing they made quite a few wrong turns and wanted to get the multiplayer mode right even though time was running out.

The next thing on Endrant's list of tasks soon as we returned to England was gutting the previous multiplayer design. It was a mess, the design focusing on parts that were either cut from the main game or went down weird gameplay alleys that were not relevant or fun. This was mostly a symptom of being passed around to so many teams with so many changes to the main game rather than any single bad decision made by one designer or team. We only had time for one shot to fix the multiplayer, and it meant ripping everything apart.

Mike Armstrong was our Tech Director and a co-founder, and he wanted to do more or less the same direction with the codebase. He wanted to unify the three codebases into one as it would be impossible to keep development in sync otherwise, fix bugs[2], and finish the near infinite other tasks if we did not complete this now. The tech being used was also less than ideal, lacking features support

---

[2] Bugs are errors during game creation that makes gameplay function incorrectly or not as intended.

for what the game actually needed to have a hope of being successful. The more we dug into what we had inherited, the more we realised the scale of the mess *Wolfenstein* had become. Thankfully our team was composed of first-person shooter and id Technology veterans, which is why we were hired by the publisher in the first place. I honestly think no other team would have a chance, but even with those advantages we were facing a serious uphill battle.

After only a few weeks, I was having a call with Activision to give an update and basically said, "Yes, we need to gut this whole thing—it's unusable... Which things?... Well pretty much all of it." After a pause, and some supporting docs sent to show why and what the upside was, we all agreed to continue. It was a major risk on our part to say these things since we were still negotiating the contract, but there was no way we were going to do this half-assed and mislead Activision by sugar coating anything. It added a monumental amount of work to everyone on the team, but I think we all stand by our decision.

Production

The plan had been laid out, we knew what to make, and although Endrant was still hiring, we had enough of the team together to get cracking. Organizing the staff and project was all achieved in less than two months. We grew fast and needed new office space, so we moved to Sevenoaks High Street into a space large enough for the current team with room to expand if necessary. The office space had been vacant for some time and after negotiations we received a decent deal with the first few months of rent being free as we paid for infrastructure upgrades (networking, server room, power). We also needed more office furniture... back to IKEA we go. IKEA is great for all things office related except one: do not cheap out on chairs. Seriously, game makers spend so much time in chairs that it's not even about comfort but health (ergonomics). All the money we saved on office furniture, etc. was basically spent on good chairs for everyone. Again, I don't regret this one bit.

Work was good, but owning and running a studio is stressful for many reasons. There are a million tasks needed to be done beyond actually making the game, and for Neil and I it was the first time we had to worry about these things. We had office personalities, bills, lawyers, and accountants to juggle in addition to my game duties as the Creative Director and Neil's as the Executive Producer. I make it sound that we were the only people working long hours or wearing multiple hats which is a total lie. Mark Fry, Matt Wilson (known as

Wils), Mike Armstrong, and Kalvin Lyle were all founders in the company, taking risks to be there and working their asses. They were all industry veterans whose reputations and livelihoods were attached to the success of the game and company—they did not have to be a part of Endrant. Add in every single hire as part of a team toiling long hours and doing amazing work while worked well together. For our first Christmas party, everyone went to a Belgian pub in London for dinner together including our significant others. All of us in attendance, smiling and having a good time when the realization struck Neil and I: we are doing it, we are making games on our own terms. I have shipped nearly 20 games in over 20 years and that was one of the most rewarding moments of my life. Of course this was the pinnacle, meaning a downwards trend would follow and end up becoming a spiral.

The reality was that the project had been running nearly five years by the time we got involved, and the amount of legacy decisions, mostly bad ones, were a real drag on what we could accomplish. Activision just wanted it "shipped" so they could draw a line under it as they had suffered as anyone else involved on this project. A great deal of the bandwidth we had as a small developer was just to get the code and gameplay salvaged. Creating something wholly new and pushing tech/design or other aspects beyond what our competitors were doing was never an option. We had to take a game that was completely unplayable and not fun, and make it at least decent. The absolutely last thing anyone wanted to do is kill the franchise so we had to hit a certain quality level. Again, thankfully some of the team had worked on the last title in the series, *Wolfenstein: Enemy Territory*, and all of the leads were familiar with the tech and had shipped at least one if not a few games using it. This project was about making the right calls and decisions rather than creating the most uber game that redefines the genre.

While part of the team was redesigning the gameplay, creating a proper class-based system with deployable gameplay elements, and building other aspects that needed to be implemented, Mike and a handful of programmers set about unifying the codebases between the platforms and identifying what we could use from the single player code plus features we had to add or support. A host of features had to be added such as deferred renderers, VOIP[3] solutions, basic items assumed would be available but weren't, to larger items like UI overhauls. After a few months, we had really pulled something together, but I was not sure we could succeed at

---

[3] VOIP = Voice Over Internet Protocol, basically being able to talk using voice through the internet.

(even though I had promised Activision), and the foundations of the game had finally been set to start actually making the game. In six months Endrant remade the entire multiplayer game, redoing all the gameplay, levels, and most of the tech... while changes to the single player gameplay impacted what we had to adjust too. Add we had to get id Software and Activision to sign off on everything, I consider this project a great accomplishment for the team.

I make it sound like the process went smoothly, but it certainly did not. There were many ...many late nights, 2 a.m. phone calls from Activision when a build seemed to not be working in QA with key features not in (they had used the wrong build) and bugs appearing that did not seem to have easy solutions while only having 12 hours to fix before a submission, etc. Some of these are issues that happen when making any game but some were not. There was one instance where the single-player maker, Raven Software, wanted to make a few changes and the schedule was going to be pushed out several months. Now for them it was important and I agree it was needed; however, what did that mean for us? We had to follow step and make changes and follow as we were "downstream", especially in design. At first Activision was reluctant to change anything, including our schedule or milestone payments. We were work for hire, they our only client at the moment. We had no negotiation power, no war chest of cash to fall back on, and our options were exceedingly limited.

We did have one card, a nuclear option that we calmly, coolly explained to them. *We could close. Yup, you are right. According to the original contract, you have NO obligation to extend extra payments to cover the extended schedule. Of course that means we cannot remain a viable business, and by UK law I have to notify my employees immediately as we need at least 90 days of funds available. Would you like me to do that? Where would you like me to send the hardware back to?* It's a shitty card to play, mostly because this was not a bluff, and also we had worked so hard to make this game fun and wanted to finish it. The extension was not because Endrant messed up. If Activision wanted the game to ship with multiplayer, they would have to bend. Endrant and Activision discussed whether or not we could ship without multiplayer, but first-person shooters, especially *Wolfenstein*, could not ship without that gameplay mode. Amendments were drawn up and signed, and we continued onwards.

The Curveball

When Endrant hit alpha and was in QA proper, we started talking to Activision in earnest about the next project. We had a few ideas that we bantered back and forth, and we had several options. Some of them were more support roles, helping out with other first-person shooters and other rather exciting possibilities. This was 2008, and unfortunately huge economic shifts were happening throughout the world, including The biggest global crash since the Great Depression which is difficult to ignore. Activision started to close studios. At first it was internal projects which extended to their partners. Our talks started to be delayed as the Publisher "sorted things out", and eventually they basically said, "We are not doing any new external development right now."

So this "pay your dues" project we were doing with Activision was not that but a painful project salvaging someone's dirty work for no light at the end of the tunnel. In fact, we were just placed into some serious jeopardy as we only had a few months of milestones left and enough cash to go a few months beyond. Even though I was upset with Activision, I knew they had invested in us and would do something about this issue if they could. Business has no loyalty but cash does, so I knew their hands were actually tied. So here we are—our new reality. We needed to ship this game still, fix the bugs, and make it great as it's Endrant's CV now while pitching new games and ideas to other publishers soon as possible.

Neil and I decided along with the founders that talking to the whole team and letting them know where things stood was the right course of action. We gave them the background information, how we got here, what we were doing, and all of our possible outcomes. This was a painful series of meetings as the team had bled to make this game work, and now we were introducing all sorts of scenarios, a few of them very bad, to these great folks. Some of them had moved house, families, purchased new places to live, etc., which weighed on my mind constantly.

Hope

Luckily between the founders, we had many game industry contacts since we had worked and shipped games for pretty much everyone. We created pitch documents for a huge variety of games and received the most traction with EA, Sony, and Codemasters.

Codemasters liked our background in the first-person shooter genre and a few of our pitches. We went to their headquarters in Leamington Spa for a series of meetings. It turned out Codemasters had IP they wanted to make into games and wanted us to create pitches around those options. Some of them were pretty cool. The Publisher had the Clive Barker's IP so lots of potential, but they also had some pretty weird stuff that sounded more like pet projects than actual good ideas; however, we were in a tight spot so we did not turn down any idea, and said we would create a few pitches. We came back with a game based on a Clive Barker book that everyone thought was cool. Right up Codemaster's alley with a combination of scary and solid shooter, we went a few rounds back and forth on the concept with them.

Unfortunately this discussion was around the time Codemaster's recent game releases were performing badly in sales and considered awful to play.. If it was not a racing game, they did poorly on it both critically and financially. Add this to the global economic recession of 2008, and we got word that they were basically only going to do racing games moving forward.

Simultaneously we were talking to Sony in Liverpool about a few new games. The first and largest was *APB: All Points Bulletin*. The game was being made on PC by developer Realtime Worlds in Glasgow. In mid-development, the game had issues and was running very late (sound familiar?). What Sony was looking at was to make a PS3 version. There were many developers bidding on making it, and Sony asked if we would like to get involved too. We reviewed the current work in progress and design docs from the PC dev to determine what we may want to do if we bid on making this version for consoles. After reading about halfway through the

303

documentation, I was quite worried. I found many holes, weird decisions that did not make any sense to me. Talking this over with my designers, Wils asked, "Surely they know this? Documentation must be out of date or something." I did not assume anything and asked Sony about these issues. The third-party did state on the latest builds[4] having a few concerns about aspects of the gameplay. I basically said, "Look, I would not implement this game on the PS3 as written at all. I want to give you a pitch that fixes the issues I see with the game, and the budget and scope will reflect that." I did not know what the other developers were doing for the pitch, but Endrant was not going to commit doing a project half-assed. They replied, "Sure, do what you think will make the best game." If nothing else, Sony had the right attitude.

The Endrant team basically rewrote the game design from scratch, taking the key elements that were awesome in the current PC design of *APB* and fixing our perceived issues with the rest. We then did the costing, budgets, and schedule outline to deliver the game. The numbers we got back scared us a bit: £13+ million, 18

---

[4] Builds are when the team compiles and puts together a full working version of the game that they have so far. The game must be built before being able to run it.

months to Beta, and needing to essentially triple our headcount to deliver the game. We decided to pull no punches and sent the pitch, being open about everything as possible. We heard back quite quickly—Sony really liked the design and the pitch, finding it solved a lot of the issues they had with the design. After reviewing the budget, Sony only asked, "Are you sure you don't need more money?" We thought the budget was on the high side and that they would balk. Apparently not. A few weeks after, we received notification from Sony that we won the bid. We were ecstatic. That sense of relief died almost immediately as Sony followed up with "But we want to see how the PC version does first before we green light this fully". I asked, "Did they sort out the gameplay questions you have? Not yet? Are they going to? Not sure?" ...Crap.

Now our future depended on a studio that we had no insights, control over, and idea if they were going to pull off their game. Sony was great though, they knew our situation and offered us some prototype work in two areas. Endrant surviving was in their best interest, but I still appreciated that they were looking out for us in any case.

The first was motion controller prototypes. The motion controllers for the PS3 had not been released yet, and they were looking for innovative gameplay that revolved around the technology. We signed all sorts of documents (e.g. non-disclosure agreements, also known as NDAs) and swore many oaths, and Sony sent us a few prototypes to play and develop ideas. These were the wand-like controllers with the ball at the end that the console uses to know the player's 3D position in real space. Lots of potential, and what could be fun?

Getting very pressed at this point, we were running out of both time and money. Endrant was only a few weeks away from giving our staff notice that they would be made redundant and need to look for work elsewhere. We did not have time to make a proper prototype using code but did come up with an innovative approach we could show off relatively easily. We created a game called *Shadowplay*.

Shadowplay was a platform game where players guide a little shadow creature by manipulating light. The PS3 motion controller was like a flashlight, and by changing the direction/angle/position players pointed it, they changed the shadows cast in each level. You ended up all over the place, shining a light to create platforms, stairs, block enemies, and activate level elements that enabled your creature reach the exit. Now saying we "completed it" is an exaggeration. We had like a week or two at most until our next meeting with Sony, and creating a proper playable prototype would be impossible. What

Endrant created was design docs, movies showing the controller in a picture display over mocked up or faked gameplay, and lastly we made a diorama... yes, an actual diorama. Since the game was made to feel like you were using a real flashlight that impacted the shadows as in the real world, we made a real level.

We bought a big, old beat up 36" CRT TV and gutted it to use the facade. We then proceeded to make Styrofoam and paper levels around the design of the basic game. Alongside we created movies of a few dozen elements, showing how it would interact with the controller and play out in mock levels. We had artist and animators working around the clock on the videos, and those who could not code or draw were assigned arts and crafts duty making this TV into a level. After building the level, we worked out how to demo the "TV" with a real flashlight to create shadows and lights for a simple level, even including our little hero on a stick to "move" around.

The day of our meeting with Sony we went to their London studio armed with memory sticks and paper printouts of the design, flashlights, and a giant TV in our arms. We had to take the train from Sevenoaks then the tube across London with our paraphernalia, and throughout the trip I was wondering "Are we crazy?" I have been part and the recipient of many project pitches but nothing quite like this.

We finally arrived and were shown into the meeting room. The looks on their faces as we set up everything was priceless—a mixture of bemusement and curiosity, and thankfully a bit of humour. We showed the documents then the movies. Sony seemed to get it, and for the time, this was an innovative use of the controller. We showed them the TV and how it would actually "feel" to play the game. I consider the fact we had a pre-existing relationship went a long way in this situation. We must have looked a bit like madmen with flashlights, and arts and crafts projects which are not normally part of a game pitch. Upon finishing the presentation, Sony asked a few good questions and seemed to understand the concept, which was the point, silly or not, since the game was both complex and simple at the same time and difficult to get across unless someone saw it in action.

Lastly and part of all these discussions was the possibility of working on PlayStation Home projects. PlayStation Home was a "location" where players logged into PlayStation to hang out. PS Home was being pushed hard at this point with support for Sony if the game had a Home location that players could check out even if not in the game. Developers did not always have time or the skills to make a Home space for their game, and Sony thought we could help create or support others in making these while we waited for *APB* or

Shadowplay to receive the green light. Sony was really going out of their way to keep Endrant's doors open, and it was greatly appreciated.

Doom

At this point our money was running out. It was an agonising few months. Everyone was working so hard to line up a project. The team was helping create pitches, Neil and I were travelling all over talking to everyone we could, but we were playing chicken with a brick wall. Neil and I went out for a coffee and had to really, objectively look at our options. Will the PC version of *APB* be any good? If not, the console version was dead in the water. Looking over the docs again, and getting an update from Sony on their thoughts regarding the most current build, I was not going to bet my company on it. What about *Shadowplay*? It was making the rounds at Sony but would take months to get going even if they decided to move forward, and we had no guarantee. Sony Home projects would be a trickle of cash coming in, not enough by itself to keep Endrant going. EA said they may have something, but give them a few weeks to sort out other projects before touching base again. Nothing definitely there. I could take out a bank loan and put more money into the company to give us a few more months, but this was 2008 and banks were not lending to small businesses, so the odds of this happening were small and only a good idea if there was definitely a project to be signed... and soon. Plus I had already invested most of my savings at the beginning so Endrant could get started—going further into debt was a huge risk.

We had two options: double down and hope that one of the two options worked out or close gracefully. Closing gracefully means give everyone three months' notice, pay bills, and close cleanly. Doubling down meant we would burn every penny, do everything possible, and if things went poorly, burn in a spectacular fashion.

Neil and I decided closing gracefully would be best as we had no guarantees, the industry was backing away from external development, and banks stopped lending. Being overly optimistic was just foolishness at this point. Gathering the founders together, we basically repeated the discussion and listened to their thoughts. We were essentially all in agreement, sad as it was. Within a few weeks of successfully shipping a multiplatform AAA[5] game, we had a team meeting that laid everything out, but this time saying by "X"

---

[5] AAA games (pronounced "triple A") are games of the highest quality, scale, and biggest budgets. Similar to the movie industry (e.g. "A" and "B" movies), this grading system stems from the beef and agricultural industry.

date we are out of money so everyone should start looking for other work. There is nothing worse—nothing. These were my friends and co-workers. They had succeeded, and we let them down. It doesn't matter that factors were beyond our control and the time scale was so short with little we could do. It did not matter that we did all we could to get more work, none of that matters, it failed, we failed them.

Next on the list was to get everyone work. Endrant reached out to the very headhunters we used a few months before to bulk up our ranks and worked with them to get our employees jobs elsewhere.

The Aftermath

The next few months are a bit of a blur. I called Sony and said, "Many thanks for trying to help us out, but in three months we are shutting down. We have started the process of laying people off and closing down properly." The people at Sony were very kind and understanding, saying all sorts of nice things about us, but if anything changed to give them a call as they wanted to work with us. We called EA next, saying the same thing and their response was similar with the added note that I should get a hold of them before starting anything else afterwards. Cryptic but ok.

The team was understandably devastated and upset, scared for their own futures. The founders did all we could to make this situation painless as possible from getting them into contact with people we knew were hiring, giving glowing references, and anything else. We at least managed to give a few months warning, and they were completely up to speed the entire time regarding the status of the company. At the same time, we were talking to bankruptcy consultancies as we had leases and other longer term commitments that were not possible to maintain. Paying off everyone we could with the staff (excluding ourselves) as the top priority. Neil and I had stopped taking pay long ago, and overall I basically worked two years for free and made loans to Endrant a few times. I like to rationalise that this experience was an education, just expensive tuition on learning how to run a development studio.

When talking to my friends and family, everyone tiptoes around like we experienced a death. The wife was understandably upset since we had spent the best part of two years and a huge part of our savings, and the studio venture clearly did not work out which put huge strains on us. Not to mention I was about to be unemployed for the first time in 18 years. I had not even begun thinking what to do next—I was neck-deep closing down Endrant, and I had no energy to even consider my future. Eight months earlier was the Christmas party high point and now most definitely the low point which was every bit as notable and extreme.

Lessons

What were the lessons learned? What would I do differently next time? This is one of the first parts of this book that is not recollection or direct experience, but actual advice.

1) Trust everyone, but cut the cards.

This means that relationships matter, and there must be some level of trust beyond general agreements. Also, understand that the people you deal with as a partner may change or other factors can occur that no one has control over. Activision hired us as work for hire with the promise of more projects afterwards. I am certain they intended to follow through, but some of the people we dealt with early on moved to other areas of the corporation, leaving new people in charge. The company also switched directions in how they were handling development which had nothing to do with us but affected us directly in the end. Unless it is in a contract, signed and done... it's not done. You must do everything to get any important aspects in writing. If it's not written, treat the agreement like it does not exist. This whole process made me a bit more cynical overall but necessary for business. It also means being a bit more of an "ass" to get your way by demanding certain things in writing. I am a collaborator by nature, and this was a hard lesson for me to learn on some levels.

2) Always be searching for work.

This is kind of linked to the above point, but any successful developers, especially smaller ones, are always chasing new work, even when they are fully tasked with existing work that lasts into the foreseeable future. When Endrant got the rug taken from under us by Activision, we were caught flat-footed. We had a few pitches created for Activision, but they were tailored for the Publisher's IP/tech needs. What did Endrant want to make if we had no restrictions? What pitches did we have ready for other publishers? What game industry contacts did we have to even get a meeting? Luckily, we knew a lot of people in the industry so we had avenues for discussion, but we still had to get the process going from a near standstill. Being new as a developer studio, Endrant did not have a huge war chest of cash set aside for a rainy day, so any delay was acutely felt. Always be chasing work to avoid this situation. If you land "extra" work that your bandwidth can't handle immediately, expand the team, delay start dates, or implement other options. Too much work is something you can deal with, not enough will kill you. Never be complacent in this area.

3) You must make hard decisions and act as a "bad guy" sometimes.

While pitching to publishers, we kept on the full development team of Endrant. We did not lay off anyone on the team until the very end and could have sooner, maybe buying ourselves another month or two. Would it have made a difference? I don't think in our particular case, but honestly, I think stating this makes me feel better. The right business call would be to lay off anyone that I could have at the point to cut costs. I am not inherently an overly nice guy but not a prick either. This is a lesson that I have the hardest time learning and accepting. To be successful at business, you must have a certain hardness, and I am not totally comfortable with this approach.

Epilogue

Now with nearly eight years between the writing of this book and the closure of Endrant, it's interesting to analyse whether we made the right decision to close or not.

APB PC ran late—like really late—and was not released until 2010. putting its developer into administration. The game was not very well received with mixed reviews. The developer did not address many of the issues we saw and questioned back in 2008, which I think contributed greatly to their problems. Bought by another publisher and retooled, it was released as a Free-to-Play game. In fact, the PlayStation version was greenlit at some point, but the game is still not released and does not have a firm date announced beyond 2016. Obviously hanging Endrant's future on landing this project in 2008 would have been even more disastrous as it would not have happened. Sony was wise to wait, and we were wise to pass.

Shadowplay's possible future is a bit harder to predict. Sony's Motion controllers were not exactly a success, and games that required them and made money were few and far between. The actual hardware was quite good and the precision surprising, but I don't think there was enough support from developers or Sony to know if the technology reached its full potential. In hindsight, I think that putting our eggs into this basket would have not paid off

EA's cryptic "come talk to us after" was interesting and lead me to where I am now. The Publisher wanted me to come in before I started anything new so I could possibly consult for them on an upcoming project. *Crysis 2* was underway, and they wanted the multiplayer to really be competitive with other first-person shooters available. Having worked on games like *Call of Duty*, *Soldier of Fortune*, *Wolfenstein*, and others, EA wanted me to come in for a few months and advise. Well that three months turned into nearly four years and three different EA titles. I have been consulting ever since for various publishers and developers, it all starting with that call. Will I stay a consultant or maybe start a new developer now armed with these lessons under my belt? Not sure yet. It's as much about opportunity and lining up projects as it is about desire or anything else.

So, what did we learn?

My goal at the start of this book was to impart the concept on how complex, large, and interconnected making games is. It takes many skilled and passionate people in every step of creation to make something that even sees the light of day, let alone something new and special.

Looking at the different groups involved—publishers, developers, press, and gamers, plus all the moving parts within them—is quite the journey to abbreviate. Each has enough depth for an entire book or several, but I wanted to give a decent overview so that you can understand what each does and the interplay between the different groups. This understanding is the number one thing most people don't see at first, and it's nearly impossible unless you are neck deep and have worked with all these types of people on an actual project. Luckily, I have done this many times with various levels of success and can pass what I learned along.

Hopefully these examples and anecdotes provide some context of not only the real facets of making games but methods and background on where these originated. A lot has changed in since the mid-1990s when I started making games, and I think being able to highlight some of those changes will help others plot out what is next and how to approach making games in the future. That said, I don't think anyone really knows where this ride is going, but at least we can make new mistakes going forward rather than repeating old ones if we spend the time learning.

The industry is ever-changing with technology eclipsed daily and huge leaps occurring every few years that change everything... again. The games industry a big business with big corporations bringing everything to the table, and it is also five guys in a basement eating pizza while working on passion projects. For every story about how something "is" there are innumerable others that will contradict it as every single game making experience is new and different.

It is hard work, incredibly rewarding, and fun - I cannot imagine doing anything else.